INSURANCE & FINANCIAL ADVISOR EDITION

IGNITE!

THE BURNING SECRETS OF EXPONENTIAL GROWTH FROM THE GREATEST EXPERTS ON THE PLANET

IGNITE!

THE BURNING SECRETS OF EXPONENTIAL GROWTH FROM THE GREATEST EXPERTS ON THE PLANET

PAUL FELDMAN

Advantage®

Published by Advantage, Charleston, South Carolina.
Member of Advantage Media Group.

ADVANTAGE is a registered trademark, and the Advantage colophon is a trademark of Advantage Media Group, Inc.

Printed in the United States of America.

ISBN: 978-1-59932-786-0
LCCN: 2017932303

This publication is designed to provide accurate and authoritative information in regard to the subject matter covered. It is sold with the understanding that the publisher is not engaged in rendering legal, accounting, or other professional services. If legal advice or other expert assistance is required, the services of a competent professional person should be sought.

 Advantage Media Group is proud to be a part of the Tree Neutral® program. Tree Neutral offsets the number of trees consumed in the production and printing of this book by taking proactive steps such as planting trees in direct proportion to the number of trees used to print books. To learn more about Tree Neutral, please visit **www.treeneutral.com.**

Advantage Media Group is a publisher of business, self-improvement, and professional development books. We help entrepreneurs, business leaders, and professionals share their Stories, Passion, and Knowledge to help others Learn & Grow. Do you have a manuscript or book idea that you would like us to consider for publishing? Please visit **advantagefamily.com** or call **1.866.775.1696.**

This book is dedicated to the two most important people in the world, my children, Emily and Sam.

I would also like to thank Steven Morelli, Christina Irene, Susan Rupe, and Matt Godbey. Without your help, this book would have never happened.

TABLE OF CONTENTS

PART II: SALES

PART III: MARKETING

INTRODUCTION

My kindergarten teacher went around the room one day and asked all the kids what we wanted to be when we grew up.

Some had the usual answers: firefighter, police officer. Others had incredible ideas about what they wanted their careers to be: a doctor, lawyer, accountant, and even astronaut.

When it came to me, I was eager with my answer: "I want to be an insurance agent!" I remember how everyone laughed and how I didn't care. Did they go into strangers' houses and offices; talk about their hopes, dreams, and fears; and offer answers to those deepest concerns? I knew early on about the magic of selling insurance. I also knew my dad had a nicer car than theirs did and that I got to do things that they didn't.

Had they ever been invited into a warehouse full of candy and told to pick whatever they wanted? I did.

Dad was my hero back then. He, like his father before him, was an insurance agent. I tagged along with him on client visits, feeling privileged to have access to the adult world and doing important things. He even used to call me his "good luck" charm. I realize now that my father probably knew that having a kid around was a good way to soften up a prospect, which sometimes worked and sometimes didn't.

It was an adventure for me, even if certain aspects would horrify parents today. For example, sometimes when my father visited clients, he would leave me in the car listening to the radio for an hour or so and not always in the best of neighborhoods around New Jersey. I usually didn't mind too much,

At the tender age of twenty-two, I was already a few years down the career path following my grandfather, Ralph, and my father, Donald.

though, because there was always lunch out. And sometimes, if he had a really good day, I could talk him into taking me to a toy store.

At one appointment in the middle of a giant warehouse complex near Newark, my father emerged from one of the larger buildings waving so excitedly at me I thought he might have discovered a new planet inside. He told me to follow him but didn't say much else. We entered a massive warehouse of candy, gum, and just about every kind of sweet sold. It was better than a new planet; this was a kid's dream world. It turns out the client was a major distributor of candy and the happy client told me that I could pick out a box of anything I wanted for being so patient. I remember walking up and down just one of the rows that had open boxes and not being able to decide. After a little pressure, I finally settled on a box of my favorite gum, Grape Bubble Yum.

After that day, I thought being an insurance salesman was just about the coolest thing ever.

My father was my first mentor, if you hadn't guessed already. Later, beyond the fun of traveling around to meet clients, the rest of my life was not all candy warehouses. Dad was a meticulous and relentless taskmaster, and wherever we lived, there was always work to do. I had more chores than any kid I knew. From splitting wood, pulling weeds, and painting, to mowing the grass and fields, the work never ended.

I developed a strong work ethic early on, and by my teens, I had developed the habit of double-checking everything I did to make sure I got it right the first time. When I first went to work for Dad's insurance agency at age nineteen, I was working under his office manager. About a month into the job, she told me how impressed she was that she had to tell me only once how to do something and I would quickly pick it up. I had certainly learned the lesson by that point.

That lesson got me started in a lifetime's search for the best ideas and insights in doing things right the first time.

Some of that hard work is hitting the books and listening to the training (the headwork). I'll admit to spending nearly a quarter-million dollars over the years on books, self-help empowerment CDs, DVDs, trainings, seminars, and mastermind groups. I wouldn't be where I am today without all of the information I have been able to gain from these sources. The best part for me is the more I learn, the more I want to learn and experience. Not only for me but for InsuranceNewsNet's more than 250,000 readers and subscribers.

In my role as publisher of InsuranceNewsNet, I've had the opportunity to speak directly to the mentors I've read over the years. I don't read fiction or watch much television, so these people are some of the biggest influencers in my life and career. Speaking to each one was an experience I never could have dreamed would happen.

I know I don't have all the answers. I also know no one person does, but mentors have invaluable expertise to build on.

This book is a snapshot of what I learned from these mentors over the years, honed specifically for the insurance and financial professional. Their collective wisdom can help guide any business owner, entrepreneur, or employee to become more successful and achieve mastery in their professional lives.

Each of the experts interviewed in this book represents the best in their field and are the ones who influenced me the most. In these interviews, I was able to dig deeper, not only to refresh my knowledge and recharge my motivation but also to personally ask the questions that still remained and share their answers with more than fifty thousand readers every month for four years.

I am offering this "best of" collection of remastered and extended interviews I did for my magazine as a tool that I hope you will read and reread for direction and understanding. This book is a product of my constant learning to improve my insight, skills, and positive frame of mind.

That last item is often critical in sales because you can get pretty beaten down by rejection and the sheer repetition of going out and earning every day. A positive attitude not only keeps you going, but it also helps you to reexamine problems and tackle them from another perspective. Oh, and for those of you who don't think you are in sales, guess again. *Everyone* is in sales; nothing happens in business until a sale is made. You sell yourself, your ideas, and your company every day. You even sell to your kids when you persuade them to clean up their room.

No matter what your issues and problems are in your work or personal life, you will find some inspiration here. Each of these interviews represents a chapter in my life, and I'm not sure I could have ever found a better way to encapsulate or share my passion for learning and understanding the world of insurance. At times, I felt like I was having a conversation with an old friend. My purpose with each of these interviews was to go "deeper" rather than "wider," and I was more interested in getting specific answers from an entrepreneur's perspective that could actually help my readers (and myself) be more successful.

Each of these experts had intense, passionate, and unique personalities. The collection of articles that resulted from our talks represents about ten to twenty hours of time each, between initial research, editing, and design. In fact, I gained so much knowledge from everyone featured in this book that it was much more difficult than I thought to summarize everything I was able to learn from them, as I always felt that I might be leaving out something incredibly profound.

I derive a bit more wisdom each time I read these interviews, so it's an honor to be a catalyst for this information.

Like my dad waving me into that sugary dream world that fateful day, it is my pleasure and privilege to open the door to this massive warehouse of ideas. Please, step inside, fill your pockets, and take these lessons with you on your journey toward self-improvement. I hope this will be as rich a wellspring of knowledge and inspiration for you as it has been for me.

CHAPTER 1
FINDING A BEGINNING

Cars whizzed by in blurs of color inches from my window while my car sat on the highway shoulder. Minutes before, I had been in that traffic, gripping the steering wheel as I worried about whether in a few days I would have to close the business I'd been nurturing for several years. Now I was parked on the shoulder, concerned that the tears welling in my eyes made it unsafe for me to drive.

This is difficult for me to talk about because I typically don't break down like that. I pride myself on not only surviving but on persevering through hard times.

My company, InsuranceNewsNet, and my family were everything to me, but it was clear I could not sustain both. After several years of struggle, I was going to let my dream go. In a few days, time would run out for me to save my business, and I would have to focus on my day job of selling vacuum cleaners (that's a whole other story).

But what brought those tears was not grief but relief. While I was driving, I received a call from someone who said he would invest in and ultimately save my company. All the ratcheting tension broke immediately and I felt like I could take my first deep breath in months.

Those were among the most difficult days in my life, but words pulled me through. Those words came from many of the people you will read about in this book. As I drove between sales appointments, I listened to cassette tapes of these authors speaking so often that I could recite along with them.

I got hooked on expert advice after reading my first Anthony Robbins book, *Awaken the Giant Within*. My own growth was scary and confusing, as it is for most of us, and advice from experts like Robbins was a source of some much-needed encouragement. When I was nineteen and had just gotten my insurance license, I knew that in order for my career to reach its fullest potential, I would need some help. It may sound a bit dramatic, but that book was an indispensable guide for me in getting the most out of both my career and my life. I guess you could say it was the kick in the butt I needed, and at just the right time, too.

The Pain That Began an Insurance Career

My formal education had ended early in college, after getting the boot at the end of my first year (and not for my grades). But Robbins's writing and the influence I had received from my father's early mentorship helped me to see that success was up to me and only me. Many people have the mind-set that they are entitled to something, but if I've learned one thing in life, it's that nothing is beneath you if it's what you need to do to survive. You have to do the hard work (even if it's menial) to gain the knowledge and experience that earns you the role and responsibility you seek.

The winter break before my expulsion, I had taken the steps to get my insurance license, so when I got kicked out of college at nineteen, the obvious decision was to go all in on the career I always knew I wanted in the insurance industry.

My dad's insurance agency had a library of about five years' worth of industry trade magazines. He told me to read them and learn the business. It was probably the most painful experience of my life because they were terribly boring, but despite that, they really were a treasure trove of information.

Over the years, I did everything at his agency. At one point I was the only employee he had. I started off basically as the receptionist, stuffing envelopes, reconciling the checking account, paying commissions, making kits, setting up databases, writing newsletters, and handling graphic design responsibilities.

Although I look like a kid who might have wandered over from a nearby wedding, that's me at nineteen attending my first insurance carrier training meeting at the American General home office. I think you'll be able to tell which one is me.

About a year after I started working for my dad, I talked him into advertising in those same trade magazines to attract agents to our brokerage business. With a limited budget, we advertised and generated thousands of agent leads over the years, all before email even existed. I knew that it took work to get people to respond, get them recruited, and get them writing a piece of business. I would follow up on good prospects for years. Mail, phone, fax, or newsletters, whatever method we had available at the time, I used it as a point of contact. Only later in that part of my career did the Internet and email start to change everything.

The Curiosity That Birthed a Company

I was always fascinated with technology. When I started working for my dad, I took it upon myself to put that fascination to use. And since there wasn't anyone else to do it, I had no choice but to figure it all out.

The knowledge I gained proved useful to the company, helping us to build out and implement our customer relations management (CRM) system (before most people knew what that meant). Those skills also helped us practice better follow-up methods to significantly increase our recruiting efforts and sales. After all, we were generating scores of new leads every month from our direct mail campaigns and from the ads that we ran in the national industry trade journals (most of which are now defunct).

Over the years, my interest turned from computers to the Internet. I was an early adopter, starting with CompuServe and AOL. I even remember having a phone-book-sized list of modem numbers that I could dial into to access message boards and information. I got hooked early and watched the dot-com bubble inflate from the beginning. All I knew at that time was simple: I wanted in.

One day in 1998, while checking where my ad was in a magazine, I started counting the other advertisers and did some rough estimates on how much money the magazine was making on those ads. I was shocked, especially because the magazine staff members didn't even write most of the content. They relied heavily on material that was contributed for free.

Later that same day, I was on hold with an insurance company and surfing MSN, which at the time was one of the most-viewed sites because it was baked into every computer running Windows. I said to myself, "I love this site; I wish there was an MSN for the insurance industry." I remember that day like it was yesterday because it started my ascent in content development and marketing.

After further analysis of other magazines, I came up with the idea of creating an online magazine where our little marketing organization would be the only one advertised on the site. It would be like having every ad page in a magazine, I thought. I was certain we would see an unfathomable increase in business if I could get a site going. That's when the light bulb went off in my head and I drew a picture of what I wanted the site to look like. Within

a few weeks, I hired a web development company and InsuranceNewsNet.
com was born.

Inspiration Divides a Family

I started InsuranceNewsNet mostly because I didn't know any better. Had
I known how hard it was going to be, I probably never would have started!
In hindsight, though, this has been a wonderful journey. I get to work with
so many smart, successful people in the industry, from the most prominent
industry associations and insurance companies to wholesalers, superstar
agents, and advisors, to my own creative and innovative employees.

I drew on the lessons that mentors have taught me to persevere and
succeed when others thought it was unlikely, if not impossible. Their inspiration and knowledge helped me to convince my dad to expand our two-state
brokerage business to a national level. Unfortunately, my dad did not share my
newfound vision for growth for long. Disagreements over how to maximize
the business's growth became more common as time went on. Eventually, the
concept of thinking big helped me decide to leave my dad's company, where
I had spent sixty-plus hours a week for seven years building relationships
with big companies and insurance agents across the nation. By the time I
left, we had contracted close to a thousand agents, either directly or through
marketing companies and agencies we had under contract.

My initial plan wasn't to rely on a news website for advertising revenue.
Rather, it was to start my own marketing organization and use it to recruit
agents. That was the business I knew, and I already had many agents who
were ready to follow me. After leaving my father's company, however, I was
served with papers from his attorney to cease and desist from recruiting. I
didn't have enough money at the time to represent myself in a lawsuit, and all
at once my dream seemed to vanish.

Despite the setback, I saw that I was going in the right direction; I would just have to take a different path. I negotiated a small loan from my then-father-in-law, for which I still owe him a deal of gratitude, and went to work building InsuranceNewsNet with the sole goal being to make a living for my family and pay the company's bills—to survive, really. Truthfully, I had nothing mapped out, because I had little idea what I was doing, much less what to expect.

Surviving by Learning, Learning to Survive

In 1999, the Internet was still a novelty. The dot-com craze was on the downslide, and hardly anyone in the insurance industry was rushing online. In fact, most of the companies I called on barely had a website, which was usually nothing more than an online brochure with little to no purpose other than to get contact information. I felt like I had skated to where the puck was going to be, only to get there before the game had even started. As a result, it was an everyday battle just to survive the first year.

In those early days, I was a one-man digital magazine and marketing company. I have no English degree; in fact, I barely passed my one English class in college. I had never studied computer science or programming either, but suddenly I was learning to code well enough to maintain the site. I didn't have the money to license news feeds or to pay for a programmer to integrate them. So I found the content I could use and pasted every article on the site for the first six months. When ads needed to be created, I figured out how to use Photoshop and designed ads for the advertisers. I was essentially learning new careers to keep my own alive, and what I learned during those years were invaluable skills I still use today.

I had a number of encouraging moments, of course, occasionally landing large lumps of ad revenue to help keep my budding family and the business afloat. But for the next year, I struggled to find many advertisers who understood the Internet. More than once, I landed myself on the verge of declaring bankruptcy and closing up shop for good.

My first lifeline came from a longtime colleague, Ray Ohlson, in the fall of 2000. Ray was the CEO of an insurance company that my father and I had done business with, and with the dot-com market heating up, he was not only fascinated with it, he was ready to invest. To this day, I don't think I ever told him that I was literally days from running out of money. The publically traded holding company that owned the insurance company he ran was probably afraid of their CEO being distracted with another business, so they decided to make the investment and became my partner. Unfortunately the dot-com bubble burst shortly after we signed the deal, and the parent company decided that they didn't want anything to do with an online business. For the next year, they did everything they could to get out of the deal and make my life miserable. Fortunately my attorney drafted up a good agreement and I ended up getting paid to take the company back in August of 2000.

Things went well for the next month until disaster struck our country when two planes flew into the World Trade Center. After 9/11, the economy and online market grew even bleaker, and in 2002, I soon found myself selling vacuum cleaners, of all things, during the day and working on InsuranceNewsNet at night—sixty to eighty hours a week, altogether, for months. I was heading to a service call one afternoon, running on fumes, when my phone rang. It was one of the owners of a mergers and acquisitions firm that was interested in a partnership with funding. We closed a deal quickly, and once again, my business was saved.

Within a couple of years, however, the partners began having issues of their own and I decided to buy them out and take control of my future. This time, I had much more knowledge, experience, and grit, which led me to succeed beyond everyone's expectation.

Lessons for *Your* Journey

The experience was a great reminder of lessons learned. I knew that stuffing envelopes, which I had been doing all my life, would result in business down the road, so I stuffed away. You have to earn your good luck.

My motto has always been: *Do whatever it takes to get the job done and don't whine about it.* Nobody is going to do it for you, especially when you own your own business. You have to take risks, be bold, and persist through failures. You can't quit when you have a setback. Think of a professional boxer. He doesn't quit when he takes a few hits to the face. When you step into the ring of life, you are going to get hit in the face. In fact, you are going to be knocked down and it's likely that it will happen many times. But it's not how many times you get knocked down; it's how you get up and continue to fight.

My business almost failed twice, but I persisted to create a multimillion-dollar-a-year publishing company. I could have quit many times. I was even told to do so by many people, including my ex-wife and family. But my pig-headed determination has carried me through a lot of setbacks and failures in life, and determination can do the same for you with the right mind-set.

During my most difficult days, some of the experts in this book kept me going and helped me to reset and recalibrate my mindset. It was immensely rewarding to re-immerse myself in their work and discuss it directly with them. And as I mentioned before, they were my rock stars, so I was even a little starstruck at times. I'm an avid listener of audiobooks, and over the years, I have worn out tapes by listening to these folks endlessly, etching their voices in my brain.

No matter how long you have been on your journey, there's always a better way, always something you can learn and be encouraged by to make the road easier. In the words of the great Jim Rohn, *"A formal education will make you a living; self-education will make you a fortune."*

PART I: LEADERSHIP

CHAPTER 2
THE UNBREAKABLE LAWS OF LEADERSHIP

John Maxwell

As my own business began to grow, sprouting from a single employee (me) to a team of salespeople, writers, designers, programmers, and account managers, leadership became an increasingly important component to managing the growth successfully.

Within the business community, though, I found that leadership was an understudied principle. Business owners' eyes often glaze over when you mention studying leadership, and the reaction of rank-and-file employees tends to be even worse. That astonishes me because whether you're a business owner, executive, project manager, or simply someone looking to take control of your own professional interactions, leadership skills are critical. What I discovered over the years was that, when pressed, most people will profess the desire to be a better leader, but few are willing to put in the hard work to become one.

Employers are so busy running their businesses and departments that they often fail to think long term when it comes to their employees. Growing your company has a lot to do with growing your employees, enabling them to take on more responsibility and lift a greater burden of your business for you. Few understand that concept better than author and speaker John Maxwell. In one of his best-known books, *The 5 Levels of Leadership*, Maxwell dictates how to become a more effective leader by inspiring others to achieve their fullest potential, regardless of position or level of leadership.

John was near the top of the list of candidates for these interviews because his work is crucial to anyone entering a position of leadership. His work on developing leadership was instrumental in enhancing my own leadership skills and integral to the development of my management team. I regularly give John's book to my employees who have the potential for growth, as the principles in the book make them better workers and my job as a business owner much easier as a result.

The beauty of *The 5 Levels of Leadership* is the book's simplicity. Many writers take simple ideas and complicate them just to fill up pages or bloviate on the obvious for the sake of inflating the author's ego. This is not John's way. He is able to explain complex issues in a simplified way so that these important lessons are easier to learn, teach, and incorporate into your everyday professional life.

John had this to say about his approach to clear and simple writing: "The really prolific, smart writers, just brilliant people disdain my simplicity. I was doing an interview on TV, and the guy looked at me, and he was talking down to me a little bit. He said, 'You know, John, I've read several of your books and they're very simple.' I said, 'That's right. They really are. It's because I'm simple.'"

John explained that the material is not complicated and there is no need for a writer to make things more complicated just to look smart or sell books. Those are not his goals—his goal is to communicate how to develop leadership qualities clearly and concisely.

"I've never taken great joy out of being confused. I've never taken great joy out of being complicated," John said. "I've always taken great joy out of understanding. I'm a communicator, not an educator. An educator takes something simple and makes it complicated, and a communicator takes something complicated and makes it simple. I'm a communicator. I have an education, but I'm not an educator."

The 5 Levels of Leadership might not be complicated, but that does not mean the five levels are easy to integrate into your daily life and personal identity. The principles of exercise and nutrition are easy enough, but that doesn't mean that the act of staying healthy is commensurately easy. Good health doesn't just happen—it must be cultivated and nurtured. The same is true of great leadership. You have to develop your "leadership muscles," but once you do, the effort will pay off in multiples.

Develop your own leadership and you can pass that knowledge along to those around you. That is the fifth level of leadership, according to John: developing other leaders. That is when you know you are succeeding as a leader—when you can effectively communicate to, not "educate," others in leadership.

A Conversation with John Maxwell

FELDMAN: *What made you focus most of your work toward leadership?*

MAXWELL: Leadership is one of my passions, and so is teaching it. I've dedicated more than thirty years of my life to helping others learn what I know about leading. The subject is inexhaustible because everything rises and falls on leadership. If you want to make a positive impact on the world, learning to lead better will help you do it.

The conclusion I came to early on is that leadership is influence. If people can increase their influence with others, they can lead more effectively. As I reflected on that, a concept for how leadership works began to crystallize in my mind, and that became *The 5 Levels of Leadership*, which took me about five years to develop.

FELDMAN: *Many people hear the word "leadership" and think that because they aren't the CEO or a manager that they are not a leader, so they don't develop the skill and basically shut down when the word is mentioned. But as you say, leadership isn't about a position.*

MAXWELL: It's very simple. Everybody is a leader. They just don't always have the position, because leadership is influence. You've got a mother with two children at home? She's a leader.

The question is not, "How do we influence somebody?" The question is, "How many do you influence?" The more people you influence, of course, the better leader you are. That's a fact. But too many people look at leadership as a noun. It's not a noun. It's a verb. *Leading*—is connecting. It's adding value. It's doing. Everybody is a leader.

I wrote a book that won a Business Book of the Year award and I was told that it won by the largest margin of any business book ever. It was so popular because it was called *The 360 Degree Leader*. It was a book on leading from the middle and influencing people above you, beside you, beneath you, all around. It worked because it was very eye opening to people. For the first time, people began to see themselves truly as a leader, even though they didn't always have a leadership position.

FELDMAN: *What would you say is the most important principle of 360-degree leadership?*

MAXWELL: I would just say that the more influential leaders of the last century weren't the highest leaders. I don't know who the most influential leader of the last century was. Mother Teresa maybe. I mean look at her. She was a little nun in Calcutta, weighed about eighty-eight pounds. Maybe it was Martin Luther King [Jr.]. He never was a senator or a president, but he was arguably the most influential man in America during that century.

When you look at influence and how it works, when people think it's title or position, all you've got to do is very quickly cite those kinds of examples. They'll say, "Oh my goodness. I never thought of it like that before," but that's exactly what it is.

FELDMAN: *How important are choices when it comes to leadership?*

MAXWELL: It's always a choice. Some blame the economy, but the economy is a fact of life. What happens to people is something they can't always change, but what happens in them, they can always control. It's attitude and how they approach things.

I was in Chicago speaking to Wells Fargo right after the financial collapse and the housing market went in the toilet. I looked at them and said, "Sixteen months ago you didn't have to work. All you had to do was answer the phone. Life was good. You didn't even have to be smart. You just had to be able to fill out papers to make money. Now all of a sudden everything is changing. You're going to have to work. You're going to have to be creative. And some will do well and some won't."

When adversity comes, it very quickly separates the people who make good choices versus bad choices. That's exactly what happens with adversity. People who make good choices during adversity look at opportunity.

I was playing golf in Michigan with Alan Mulally, the CEO of Ford, who is probably without any question one of the three top CEOs in the world today with what he's done at Ford. We were talking about leadership challenges and he said, "John, I like to call them leadership opportunities because every problem has an opportunity. I've always found that problems are the greatest seed to doing well and making it big."

That's all choice. The way Alan looks at it is, "My goodness. I've got an opportunity here." Most people just say, "Dear God, might as well close up shop. Things are terrible." It's a choice.

FELDMAN: *You've said that you didn't like rules when you were young, yet all of your books center on rules. How did you learn to accept and write rules?*

MAXWELL: I still don't like rules. I like principles and laws. Rules work only in certain situations. Principles work in most situations. Laws work in every situation.

FELDMAN: *Is there a principle or law that you really struggle with?*

MAXWELL: I have to remind myself of the law of reflection every day, which basically says reflection lets growth catch up with us. The reason I do that is because I think most leaders have a bias to action. They love to have something happening. If something's not happening, they go kick it over.

Every day I have to say, "John, action is not the key. The key is reflection," because experience is not the best teacher, even though people say it is. It's the most expensive teacher, but it's not the best teacher. If experience were the best teacher, as people got older they'd automatically get better.

Evaluated experience is the best teacher. In other words, having the experience and then reflecting on it, thinking about it, and evaluating it, that's where you learn. You don't learn from the experience. You learn from taking time to reflect. So it's a great law. It just reminds me every day that no matter how much I love the action, I've got to slow down and do some reflection, make sure that I'm thinking correctly and learning from what I'm experiencing.

FELDMAN: *In your book,* The 15 Invaluable Laws of Growth, *you used the quote, "The wise man questions himself, the fool others." This is really a powerful statement because a lot of people are quick to question others rather than themselves.*

MAXWELL: That's very common. In earlier years, when I was less mature, I thought because I was a leader I had to have answers, so I was kind of like an answer man. But then as I matured I realized I really didn't have answers. I was just faking it until I made it.

So I began to ask more questions as I became confident and secure. Secure people question themselves and ask questions. It doesn't rob them of their security. They just know that that's the only way they're going to learn. Insecure people only want answers and want to provide answers. They don't want the questions.

FELDMAN: *What are some of the choices you've made in life that have had a material impact on your success?*

MAXWELL: When I was sixteen and an underclassman, I was named captain of my high school basketball team. I wasn't even the best player. I was probably the second-, maybe even the third-best player.

THE 15 INVALUABLE LAWS OF GROWTH

1. The Law of Intentionality – Growth Doesn't Just Happen. To reach your potential and become the person you were created to be, you must go out of your way to seize growth opportunities.

2. The Law of Awareness – You Must Know Yourself to Grow Yourself. Seek what you were put on this earth to do, then pursue it with all your effort.

3. The Law of the Mirror – You Must See Value in Yourself to Add Value to Yourself. Self-esteem is the single most significant key to a person's behavior.

4. The Law of Reflection – Learning to Pause Allows Growth to Catch Up with You. Investigate, Incubate, Illustrate.

5. The Law of Consistency – Motivation Gets You Going, Discipline Keeps You Going. Small disciplines repeated with consistency every day lead to great achievements over time.

6. The Law of Environment – Growth Thrives in Conductive Surroundings. Do all you can to grow yourself and create the right environment for others to grow.

7. The Law of Design – To Maximize Growth, Develop Strategies. Predictably achieve goals with a system of specific, orderly, repeatable principles and practices.

8. The Law of Pain – Good Management of Bad Experiences Leads to Great Growth. Facing difficulties is inevitable. Learning from them is optional.

9. The Law of the Ladder – Character Growth Determines the Height of Your Personal Growth. Focus on being better on the inside than on the outside. Character matters.

10. The Law of the Rubber Band – Growth Stops When You Lose the Tension Between Where You Are and Where You Could Be. Like rubber bands, we are most useful when we are stretched.

11. The Law of Tradeoffs – You Have to Give Up to Go Up. Learn to see tradeoffs as opportunities for growth.

12. The Law of Curiosity – Growth is Stimulated by Asking Why? Explore, ask questions, evaluate what you find. Repeat.

13. The Law of Modeling – It's hard to Improve When You Have No One But Yourself to Follow. Choose your role models and mentors carefully; their values will become the basis for yours.

14. The Law of Expansion – Growth Always Increases Your Capacity. Stop doing the expected and start doing the unexpected.

15. The Law of Contribution – Growing Yourself Enables You to Grow Others. Be inspired. Be inspiring.

The coach looked at the other players and said, "The reason John is the captain is because he has the best attitude on the team." I'm a sixteen-year-old kid sitting on a hardwood basketball floor thinking, "My attitude is going to determine a lot about my success." So I made a choice that I'd always have a good attitude and that stuck with me.

At fifty-one, when I had a heart attack, I said, "Wait a minute. This is too young to die." I made a choice. I'm going to eat better and exercise more, lose some weight, and do what I need to do to get my health back to where it was. That's a choice. A fact of life is that I had a heart attack. The choice is I decided to do everything I can to prevent it from happening again.

FELDMAN: *Going through your 5 Levels of Leadership book, I try to picture myself,* *and it seems like, at my own company, I'm at different levels with different people. How do you stay on one level consistently?*

MAXWELL: You don't. On *The 5 Levels of Leadership* it's very simple: You're not on the same level with everybody. So what people do is, they try to get to one level and say, "That's the level I'm on with everybody," and that's not true at all. You have to have people that you lead. The only place you're on the same level with everybody is level one, position level. You have the title, position, that's the only place you're the same.

As you go up those levels, you lose people. Not everybody is relational, so not everybody is going to go to level two with you. You've got people that work for you who probably don't even like you. So you're not going to take all of them to level two. If you take eight to level two, you're not going to take all those people up to level three.

THE FIVE LEVELS OF LEADERSHIP

| LEVEL 5: PINNACLE |
| LEVEL 4: PEOPLE DEVELOPMENT |
| LEVEL 3: PRODUCTION |
| LEVEL 2: PERMISSION |
| LEVEL 1: POSITION |

You have to set yourself. You cannot help somebody until you know what level you're on with them and then you develop strategy to get to the next level. We all rise together.

FELDMAN: *What is the most important thing a leader can do?*

MAXWELL: That's very simple. You have to add value to people. Leadership is influence. And how do you gain influence? By adding value to people. The more people you add value to, the greater your influence. That's a fact. So I tell people: don't try to be a leader. Just try to add value to people. If you add value to people, you'll gain influence with them. If you gain influence with them you'll be leading them, whether you think you are or not. So intentionally adding value to people is huge.

As Max Depree says, the leader is the servant who removes the obstacles that prevent people from doing their jobs. What a great description. That kind of mind-set requires maturity. It means coming to work every day placing other people first in our thoughts and actions. It means asking, who can I add value to today, and what can I do for others? That is not the mind-set of an immature leader. It is the mind-set of a people developer.

FELDMAN: *What is the greatest enemy of leadership?*

MAXWELL: I think it's insecurity. I think people who are insecure in leadership do great damage to themselves and the people that they lead. The greatest hindrance to great leaders is people who have leadership positions but they're highly insecure, because instead of adding value to people they want people to add value to them.

So they're always detracting. A leader should be a plus in people's lives, not a minus.

Final Thoughts

After talking to John, something was confirmed for me: leadership isn't something you're born with. It's something you develop. Influencing others is something we learn through experience, but if you don't look honestly at what worked and what didn't, the full potential to grow from the experience will never be realized. Like John said, reflection allows growth to catch up to us. That's not easy, of course. Looking back isn't something most leaders are taught to do, as so much of business training is about looking forward and always "making progress."

But progress isn't just about leading. A good leader has the right team around them to make progress possible. A bad leader tries to do everything themselves, and the company stagnates because of their ensuing exhaustion. You can't do everything yourself and be effective. It's just not possible. A good leader focuses on what they're good at and works to improve those skills. The skills they're not good at they hire for or recognize in the strengths of their staff and work to support them.

A person, whether a leader or a worker, can't develop into something that he or she is not. They can only make some improvements. On a scale from one to ten, John believes that the magic number is seven. If you're a three at something, what's the best you're going to get yourself up to? A level five? You're still not good at it, and you've wasted all that time and energy to become average instead of taking an average-level skill and making it great. Leaders shouldn't want people trying to develop a skill that isn't important to their purpose. If they're not going to handle public relations, for instance, why have them develop that skill?

It's especially difficult for those of us who aren't used to communicating with a team and collaborating with others to discover these solutions. I remember at one point early in my company's history when one of my first salesman approached me with a problem about closing business. He said to me, "Paul, I need you to work with me on this." That took me by surprise and I honestly didn't know what to do or say. I was so used to hunting alone, as most solopreneurs do when they start their business, that I had no idea how to coach someone else. But as your company begins to grow and develop, you must create processes that connect your team to your vision of purpose and train your people on how to reach the goals around that vision.

Over time, and with plenty of ups and downs, I have since become a much better trainer of people by systematizing my business. Using a system of training processes helped me to transfer my passion to the people that work for me, which subsequently enabled them to find new meaning in their jobs and in the company as a whole.

You have to take the time out to think about what a person's job is really going to be and how it connects to the bigger picture. If you can define their position's purpose at the highest level, then you can better describe what you expect of them and why. And the better you can describe their individual purpose, the better you can set them up for success by giving them fundamental training along the way.

Key Takeaways

Leadership is not a position. It is influence, and to influence someone is to add value to that person. So don't focus on trying to lead. Don't even focus on trying to influence. Simply focus on adding value to people. Remember, this goes for those below you, at your level, and even above you. That's 360-degree leadership.

Being a great leader involves choice. Rather than having a negative attitude, see problems as opportunities. The choices you make during adversity will define you as a leader. Choose to stay positive and optimistic and choose to solve the "opportunities" that come about.

Reflection is critical to growth and advancement as a leader. Experience alone does not make a great leader. It's how you reflect on experience that helps you grow. Constantly question yourself.

CHAPTER 3

HOW ADVISORS CAN MAKE THE LEAP FROM GOOD TO GREAT

Jim Collins

When I hear the word *great*, Jim Collins is the first thing that comes to mind. With a quarter of a century of relentless research, Jim has authored and coauthored six books that have sold more than ten million copies worldwide. He has truly made a science out of greatness, dedicating much of his career in scientific research to determining why some companies succeed and others fail.

The phrase "good to great" has been a staple of the business world ever since Jim published his book of the same name in 2001. The book analyzed data to track the success of companies and determine the reasons that some companies achieve sustained success when others do not.

For *Good to Great*, Jim, a former Stanford University business professor, had a team of twenty people put in fifteen thousand hours of research to find companies' secrets for success. Out of the book's three hundred pages, eighty-two are devoted to appendices and notes on the research methods. Hence, the science of greatness.

For his latest book, *Great by Choice*, Jim's objective for the nine years of extensive research was to answer the question, "Why do some companies thrive in uncertainty, even chaos, and others do not?"

Jim definitely has the academic credentials for such data-intensive research. He started his work as a researcher and faculty member at Stanford University's Graduate School of Business and expanded on this work at a management lab he founded in Boulder, Colorado. What has made *Good to Great* so popular and, well, great, is not just the data but that the book doesn't get bogged down by the technical data and analysis that buoys his findings. The book eschews an academic audience in order to target the business community. Jim made the work approachable by a general audience without dumbing the book down.

In business, as in all things, successes and failures have lessons for us. Jim has made it his work to analyze and organize this data, which he has been doing for twenty-five years now. Thanks to his books, we have this useful information organized and readily available. Jim's body of work, which includes five books so far, is essential reading for anyone who wants to build a company or team capable of outperforming the competition.

For years, I have referred to Jim's concepts in our company and executive meetings. From the flywheel to the hedgehog to firing bullets, the concepts outlined in his work have helped us define who we are as we make the move from an idea to a business and then from a business to a company. In Jim's 2011 book, *Great by Choice*, he analyzes the core competencies of the CEOs of companies that outperformed their competitors by at least ten times, or 10x. He found that these super-successful CEOs all exhibit the same core behaviors, which we explore in the following interview. Some of the results may surprise you.

A Conversation with Jim Collins

FELDMAN: *A lot of our readers have read your work—from* Built to Last, Good to Great, How the Mighty Fall, *to your newest book* Great by Choice. *Can you tell us about* Great by Choice, *and what are some of your latest discoveries?*

COLLINS: I have had the privilege to be on a journey for almost twenty-five years now. In 1988, I began this journey of trying to address one really big question: What makes a great company tick?

That journey began by teaching a course on entrepreneurship and small business for the MBA program at Stanford. The course syllabus said something along the lines of, "This is going to be a course on the unique challenges of small business or the small enterprise." And I somehow had the instinct to change the syllabus intro to say, "This is going to be a course about how to turn a small business into an enduring, great company." So I put a period at the end of that and that was the opening line of the syllabus.

Then I realized that I didn't really know very much about what it took to build an enduring, great company. And I was fascinated with the journey by which people started with a small business and built a great company out of it. So I began this long research journey, and I now can think of it as a black box and inside this black box are the distinguishing principles that separate a great enterprise from others.

In a way, you can kind of think of it as it's really almost four volumes of one question as opposed to four different volumes, the first being *Built to Last*, which looked at very long-term success; *Good to Great*, which is about how you take a good enterprise and continually work toward making it great; *How the Mighty Fall*, which looks at the dark side of how companies self-destruct or how they can self-destruct; and then finally this last one, *Great by Choice*, which is all about thriving in chaos and uncertainty and why some do and others don't.

There has always been this lurking point that led toward this. We're in a world that is going to be full of changes that we can't predict and some of them are very big, very disruptive, very fast moving, and very dangerous.

LESSONS FROM *GREAT BY CHOICE*

Discipline and Self-Reliance:

- 10Xers remain productively paranoid in good times, recognizing that it's what they do before the storm comes that matters most. Since it's impossible to consistently predict specific disruptive events, they systematically build buffers and shock absorbers for dealing with unexpected events. They put in place their extra oxygen canisters long before they're hit with a storm.

- The 20-Mile March builds confidence. By adhering to a 20-Mile March no matter what challenges and unexpected shocks you encounter, you prove to yourself and you enterprise that performance is not determined by your conditions but largely by your own actions.

- On the one hand, 10Xers understand that they face continuous uncertainty and that they cannot control, and cannot accurately predict, significant aspects of the world around them. On the other hand, 10Xers reject the idea that forces outside their control or chance events will determine their results; they accept full responsibility for their own fate.

- It's what you do before the storm hits—the decision and disciplines and buffers and shock absorbers already in place—that matters most in determining whether your enterprise pulls ahead, falls behind, or dies as a result.

Unexpected Findings:

- The 10X cases took less risk than the comparison cases yet produced vastly superior results.

- The 10X winners were not always more innovative than the comparison cases. In some cases they proved to be less innovative.

- Contrary to the image of brazen, self-confident, risk-taking entrepreneurs who see only upside potential, 10X leaders exercise productive paranoia, obsessing about what can go wrong. They ask questions like: What is the worst-case scenario? What are the consequences of the worst-case scenario? Do we have contingencies in place for the worst-case scenario? What's the upside and downside of this decision? What's out of our control? What if...?

- 20-Mile Marchers have an edge in volatile environments; the more turbulent the world, the more you need to be a 20-Mile Marcher.

FELDMAN: *Do you see change happening faster nowadays?*

COLLINS: If you look at the amount of change that happened from the end of the 1800s through the twentieth century, it has been dramatic. We had the dissemination of electricity; the rise of pharmaceuticals, television, radio, and the Internet; and, of course, nuclear weapons. You had two world wars. You had the Cold War. You had the rise and fall of an entire empire. I mean just extraordinary amounts of change, even the rise of the modern corporation is one of the changes of the twentieth century—capital markets as we know them today. The amount of change has just been utterly astonishing.

So I'm very skeptical when people say today is uniquely full of change as opposed to what people before us have faced. I do see two things, though. One is that people believe that the rate of change is faster and the degree of disruption is larger. So if they believe that and they're starting from that point of belief, then you still need to be able to answer for them, "Okay, I don't know if you're right or if you're wrong on that. What I do know is that if you believe that, we need to know what principles allow you to do well in a changing world when you're starting from that point of view."

The second is that I do believe that technological change is happening at a very accelerated pace. I don't know if it's more dramatic, but it might be happening faster.

FELDMAN: *Right. You think about the iPad, how that's just taken off and now tablets are a part of almost everyone's life in the business world. So that is good change for many people, but good or bad, how do people survive constant change and disruption?*

COLLINS: My coauthor, Morten Hansen, and I asked, "Why do some thrive in uncertainty and even chaos and others don't?" That was really the genesis of the study.

This study distinguishes itself from the prior three in two ways. The first is that it deliberately selected subjects by the severity of the environment. There are companies that outperformed their industries by ten times but didn't make it into the study because they weren't in a turbulent enough environment.

The second is that this study, more than the others, puts an emphasis on the small business and the entrepreneur, because in order to qualify for the study you had to have started your journey to be a 10x great company from a position of being small or young. Very significant companies were once start-ups. Intel had three people. MGM started in a tilt-up building in Thousand Oaks, California. Microsoft started with five people in Albuquerque, New Mexico. Peter Lewis took over his very, very small family insurance business in Cleveland and it grew into Progressive. They were start-ups and then they went on to become these great winners.

More than we did in the previous studies, we made our deliberate selections by looking at them when they were small and what they were doing then.

FELDMAN: *One of the things you talked about in* Great by Choice *is the core competencies that need to exist to be what you call a 10x leader. For a small business owner, what does it take to become a 10x leader, and how do you position yourself for that?*

COLLINS: One of the things that I found really fascinating is that most of what it takes seems to be learnable. We tend to think that somebody who would lead an enterprise to be ten times better than its industry must be a superhero. They must be off the charts with charisma and sheer brilliance and we could never learn to be like them. We actually found that the distinctive behaviors, the things that separated them, are learned capabilities and behaviors.

In the book, we use this pair of explorers, Roald Amundsen and Robert Falcon Scott, as an analogy because here you have the ultimate sort of small enterprise. They were two small teams both trying to achieve something great in 1911, to be the first to the South Pole and get back alive in a very unforgiving and uncertain environment.

The analogy to being a small businessperson out there in the world, which is so much bigger than you and potentially unforgiving, is a little bit like being Amundsen and Scott out there on the Antarctic plateau in 1911.

The way to think of it is this triangle that we put in the book. One of the points is the notion of utterly fanatic discipline. The second is this empirical creativity, and the third is productive paranoia. In the middle is this idea of level-five ambition animating the whole thing.

10X LEADERSHIP

10Xers embrace a triad of core behaviors. Animating these three core behaviors is a central motivating force, Level 5 ambition.

FELDMAN: *In the first part of your triangle, when you said "Utterly Fanatic Discipline," why use the word "fanatic"?*

COLLINS: All the people we studied were utterly fanatical about understanding what it is that they were trying to do and clearing away everything that got in the way of that. These people were truly driven, intense, and fanatically disciplined people.

Fanatic discipline means consistency of action, values, goals, service and execution, and consistency of hitting your own self-imposed performance expectations. They don't come from outside. They come from inside. You drive yourself harder than anyone else could possibly drive you.

That notion of discipline has shown up in all of our work, but it really stood out in this study and came to life in this thing we came to call the twenty-mile march. The idea of the twenty-mile march is that you're on a long journey. You mentioned earlier that many of your readers have been in business for decades, and it's a long journey. It doesn't happen overnight. You don't build a great set of customers overnight. You don't build a business that serves its particular community so well overnight. It's a journey.

What we found is that Roald Amundsen exemplified this and called it the twenty-mile march. It doesn't matter whether it's good or bad weather. You basically say, "Every day we're going to hit some allocated amount of miles toward our goal," rather than if it's good conditions going as far as we can and in bad conditions holding back. The idea of having a twenty-mile march is something that you just stay on with incredible consistency.

FELDMAN: *So how does this apply to our readers?*

COLLINS: Progressive Insurance is not exactly your insurance world, but I think it really highlights the idea of the twenty-mile march. Peter Lewis at Progressive said, "Look, we need a mechanism to keep us focused on the core discipline of our business," and that's the combined ratio for an insurance company, the core profitability. "We're not going to try to make money by a whole bunch of sophisticated investing stuff. We're going to do insurance well, and price risk well, and the real nuts-and-bolts management of that. So we're going to average a 4 percent combined ratio and we're going to have a positive profitability in that core underwriting activity every single year if we can," and they did it for twenty-seven out of thirty years—incredible consistency year in and year out.

Now, it could be that your twenty-mile march is, "I'm going to place five calls a day no matter what. I don't care if I have 105-degree temperature or whether it's a great day and I could make thirty calls. I'm going to do five a day, every single day, no matter what." That's a twenty-mile march, and whatever your twenty-mile march happens to be, you know what it is.

The twenty-mile march gives you something to focus on and to make progress on day in and day out. You have this clarity and incredible commitment to find a way of navigating your way in a world that just seems to be swirling all around you.

The discipline is in every single day you wake up, and the first thing you do is track your hours from the day before, and you do it every day, and you do it 365 days a year, and you stay on target.

The learned behavior is to say, "I need to know as an agent or an advisor, what is really the right kind of march for me?" And then they need to hold themselves to it fanatically. There's no acceptable reason for missing it, no matter what. That's what the twenty-mile march is all about.

FELDMAN: *What is your twenty-mile march?*

COLLINS: My own march is an annual one, and I track my time. Every day I put my time in a spreadsheet broken into three categories: creative time, teaching time, and other. Over time it needs to be more than 50 percent creative. 50/30/20 should be the target. And if other time starts growing beyond 20 [percent] or creative starts falling below 50, I'm off my march.

Now there are some days that are all teaching, some days that are other, whatever. But over the course of a year, I track [my time] every day and then I have a constant running monthly total, and then I have the annual total. Over the course of a year, I should really come in on target, and the only way I can come in on target is if I'm constantly making sure that I am allocating time for creative work.

FELDMAN: *What does "creative time" look like for a salesperson or business owner? Our readers' creative time is very different from yours because you create a lot of research, books, and writing. But for people who are selling insurance, what would their creative time be?*

COLLINS: I wouldn't suggest that somebody should have my march. Mine came out of asking my stepfather, who was a great physics professor in terms of great teaching, great research, and great service to the university. I once asked him, I said, "What marks a great professor?" He said, "Well, the key is you do 50/30/20. Fifty percent of your time in intellectual work, 30 percent of your time teaching, and 20 percent in other things you need to do to help the institution."

"THE KEY TO A TWENTY-MILE MARCH IS HOW YOU'RE ALLOCATING YOUR TIME AND BEING UTTERLY, FEROCIOUSLY CONSISTENT IN HOW YOU DEPLOY..."

I just wrote that down and I thought, once I formed my own research lab, I needed to stay on that track. I needed to stay on that 50/30/20. So that's where it came from.

Now if I were in a different activity in life, then I would have a different allocation. Mine might be 40 percent sales marketing, 40 percent service, 20 percent other.

The key to a twenty-mile march is how you're allocating your time and being utterly, ferociously consistent in how you deploy on the things that you know over time are the most important and tracking it.

The beauty of the twenty-mile march is when the world is melting down on you in difficult times with tremendous uncertainties, it gives you something to make sure that you're paying attention to when you wake up in the morning.

FELDMAN: *Let's talk about the second part of the triangle, the "Empirical Creative Side." What does that mean to salespeople who might not think they are creative?*

COLLINS: The people we studied were not just creative. They were really good at figuring out what works empirically. They would try things. We call it firing bullets, then cannonballs. If you're going to try something radically new that you haven't tested, you can't fire a big, uncalibrated cannonball first, because then you won't have any gunpowder left if it misses.

So fire bullets. When I see that the bullets are actually on target with something and I've got a calibrated line of sight, then I put a lot of resources behind that line of sight and fire a cannonball.

Now for a small-businessperson with limited resources, this is an extremely important idea because you always feel that you need to be thinking about doing something new, whether it's a new way of reaching your customer audience or responding to challenges. But you have to place your big steps on sound footing.

We write in the book about how Robert Falcon Scott, who didn't get to the pole first and died along with all of his people on the way back, had placed a big bet on these things called motor sledges, which were engine-driven tractors that they hadn't tested for the conditions of the South Pole. The engine blocks cracked and that led to a series of things, such as using ponies, which also didn't work.

Amundsen said, "That's not proven yet and we're betting our lives out here," and he went and lived with Eskimos. The Eskimos said, "Dogs and sleds and skis work really well out here."

The difference between the two of them is that Amundsen formulated his path based upon real proven empirical experience. He learned from the Eskimos and his own trial and error, whereas Scott went with something that was unproven.

So what does that mean for a small-businessperson? You can't afford to fire a lot of uncalibrated cannonballs. You're small. And at the same time, you have to be moving forward and doing new things because the world around you is changing.

So when you're facing questions such as, "Should I do something with social media? Should I do something with the Internet? Should I do something with whatever," instead of having this big yes or no answer, which can be paralyzing, turn it into a different question such as, "How can I fire a bullet on this? Is there some way I could do this in a small shot and see if it works?"

FELDMAN: *The third part of your triangle is "Productive Paranoia." Why is this important to 10x leaders, and how do you manage it productively?*

COLLINS: Our people were really paranoid. They worried constantly about what the world could do to them. Our leaders carried extra cash. They always assumed that they might have to go through a very difficult period. They always assumed that that period might last a lot longer than anybody anticipated.

As a result, they could stay on their march and keep moving forward, when others who are less conservative and less disciplined in good times would find themselves more exposed and maybe have to stop their march altogether.

When you put those three behaviors together, the fanatic discipline, empirical creativity, and productive paranoia, those are the three distinctive behaviors.

FELDMAN: *You have "Level 5 Ambition" in the middle of your triangle. Can you tell us what it means and how that fits in the middle of this great success pyramid?*

COLLINS: All the best people we ever studied were always trying to do something that was more than just their own personal success.

Think about what allows you to do a twenty-mile march, find and validate new things that will work even better, protect your flanks from the productive paranoia and all the things necessary to produce the best possible results you can over a long time. If it's just about some personal success and it's not really about contribution to something larger than yourself, it's very hard to sustain it.

Our leaders always saw themselves in service to some cause.

FELDMAN: *So basically you need a total mission of service to choose to be what you call "great"?*

COLLINS: Absolutely. Whatever it was, they were in service to it. So when they woke up in the morning, the question wasn't, "How do I make myself more successful?" The question was, "How can I be of better service? And how can I be of better service to whatever cause it is that I'm engaged in?"

One of the things that's very interesting about great entrepreneurs over time is you think about four phases of an entrepreneurial business. First phase, you have an idea. The second phase is converting that idea into a business, so now you have a business.

Then you might actually convert that from a business to a company. It doesn't have to be a big company, but it's a company. Then finally, you create a movement, like, "Hey, there are a lot of people who need what we do." Or, "The world will be better off because of what we do." That's a movement. I think that when you have that orientation it just allows you to be self-propelled for a very, very, very long time.

Final Thoughts

As Jim and I discussed, the core competencies of these "superleaders" can be grouped into these categories: Productive Paranoia; Empirical Creativity; Fanatic Discipline; and most importantly, "Level 5 Ambition."

To be honest, I hadn't given *Level 5 Ambition* much thought when I read *Great by Choice*. This may come as a surprise to those who have read the book because the concept of Level 5 Ambition is central to every chapter. But I was already a successful business owner and entrepreneur, so I thought of myself as sufficiently ambitious and never paid much thought to the concept. I may have already been "good to go" in the ambition department, but I was still finding my feet as a business leader at the time I started studying Jim's work. In fact, he was one of the first people I turned to for leadership advice when I started to feel like InsuranceNewsNet was growing beyond my leadership skills.

By the time I read *Great by Choice*, I had already defined Jim as an expert on strategic, big-picture management and the science of success more than anything else. I wanted a cut-and-dry, objective-based kind of education on leadership, and Jim was the go-to guy for that kind of advice. At least that's what I thought.

It wasn't until our interview that I realized I had misunderstood one of the most important findings in his research—and to leadership in general. When I asked Jim to define what he meant by Level 5 Ambition, his response shook me. Come to find out, it wasn't the kind of ambition I had interpreted it to be at all. "All the best people we ever studied were always trying to do something that was more than just their own personal success," he said. "Our leaders always saw themselves in service to some idea or ideal or cause or purpose or goal."

That clicked with me immediately. These leaders knew their mission of service and so did everyone in the company. Great leaders "channel their ego and intensity through something larger and more enduring than themselves." This behavior attracts great talent and creates a passionate workforce, and when you accomplish that, your team can achieve things you may not have considered possible, things that are probably not possible without a team buoyed by great leadership. If the core of every 10x company has an intense drive with a clear mission and purpose, then mine had to be more than my own personal drive to succeed.

After some reflection, I found my mission of service not just in my employees, customers, and their families but also in knowing that our efforts help support our customers' employees and customers and their families, too. Jim helped remind me that our service supported a chain of beneficiaries. I take a lot of pride in that purpose, and it continues to drive us to this day.

Great leaders train themselves and learn to provide that drive for their followers. It propels decisions and clears the path for success. Longevity will depend upon your ability to orient yourself with the idea of serving a cause, not with fueling personal success. So my question to you is this: What is your mission of service?

Key Takeaways

TWENTY-MILE MARCH

Work to set up a ratio that correlates the amount of time you spend each day with the category of necessary activities (e.g., 40 percent for sales, 40 percent for marketing, etc.). As you set up your ratio, allot the amount of time each percentage represents. Also set clear goals of what you mean to accomplish each day, week, month, and/or year. Then be consistent and exact, no matter how hard or easy—do no less and no more than your daily goal.

COLLINS'S TRIANGLE

1. Fanatic Discipline: Maintain a consistency of action, values, goals, service, and execution for success. The regularity you show in reaching and surpassing your own performance expectations will be a key determining factor in your overall leadership success. As a leader, you must be your own engine to drive the team and company forward.

2. Empirical Creative Side: Be creative and always be thinking of new ideas to advance your business, but fire bullets, not cannonballs, when it comes to testing new ideas. Only move forward with a new idea once you've proven it'll work.

3. Productive Paranoia: Always stay on your toes, even in good times. Especially during the good times, be conservative. Leaders who think more about what could go wrong are much more prepared when they do go wrong. Remember, Collins's Triangle doesn't work without Level 5 Ambition. Find a greater cause to serve rather than just your own personal success. The most successful leaders have this noble drive in common.

CHAPTER 4
UNLEASH YOUR LEADERS

Ken Blanchard

When it comes to leadership, there are few with the experience, know-how, and proven track record that Ken Blanchard possesses. His company employs more than four hundred people, but he does not consider himself the chief executive officer of the company so much as, to use his language, the "chief spiritual officer." Spirituality is central to Ken's personal and professional self. His goal is to inspire his team to push themselves, which is a leadership skill I'm sure we would all like to improve upon.

In speaking with Ken, he exuded passion and a sense of generosity that seemed to transfer to everyone around him. It's a trait that he's made part of his managerial philosophy, and he's found that it doesn't just make for happy employees, but it also inspires a working environment that stimulates growth.

Just as he shares this message with his team, Ken uses his writing to share this message with others. His best-selling book, *The One Minute Manager*, coauthored with Spencer Johnson, has sold more than thirteen million copies and remains on bestseller lists along with titles such as *Raving Fans, Gung Ho!,* and *Whale Done!* Thirty years after publication, *The One Minute Manager* still sells a couple hundred thousand copies a year.

What is Ken's message? He wants managers to be bearers of hope. He wants managers and employers to view employees not as subservient underlings but as true partners. It is all too easy for a manager or business owner to neglect the growth and motivation of the people who work hard to make the business happen on a daily basis. That's why Ken stresses that his one-minute leadership and management process is not something a manager imposes on his team but rather a process that a manager does *with* them.

And the process works. Ken's philosophy has enabled his company, which he founded with his wife in 1979, to be named by the San Diego Union-Tribune as "The Best Place to Work" in San Diego in 2013. For all of his success, Ken is a humble and thoughtful man whose influence has helped me soften my own management style. In this interview, Blanchard shares in-depth insights into what defines the best leaders, how to hire winning employees, ideas on boosting sales, the power of sales mentoring, and much more.

A Conversation with Ken Blanchard

FELDMAN: *Most of our audience consists of what you could consider small businesses. You have been involved in developing people management and leadership skills for almost thirty years now. What are some key traits that make or break today's leaders and business owners?*

BLANCHARD: There are three things you must focus on. First, you have to be a bearer of hope. My title in our company is chief spiritual officer. I leave a message every morning for everybody in our company. I do three things: I tell them who to pray for because people tell me about anyone who needs prayers. We have amazing data in fifteen years on the power of prayer. Second, I praise unsung heroes, people who are really going out of their way but who aren't out front. And then, finally, I leave them an inspirational message about what I've been reading and what I've been thinking. The main goal is to keep them pumped up, to keep them tied into our vision. I asked Max DePree, who was the legendary chairman of Herman Miller. He said, "I have to be like a third-grade teacher. I have to say the vision and values over and over and over again until people get it right."

The second key trait is your ability to view employees as business partners. The biggest problem I've seen with entrepreneurs is that they sometimes feel they are the only ones with the brains, and their people are, in the traditional sense, hired hands. For example, we were down 29 percent in 2009. We projected $60 million, and we realized that if we got $48 million we would be lucky. During a two-day meeting, we divided our three-hundred-plus employees into small groups. Half of the groups looked at cutting costs and the other half focused on increasing revenues. And so we actually ended up doing $48 million in 2009, yet we didn't let anybody go, because we had so many great suggestions on cutting costs, including people taking salary cuts and stopping 401(k) matches. So you have to treat your people as your business partners. Stop meeting behind closed doors and making decisions there.

Finally, you've got to be a servant leader. And when I mention servant leadership, people think I am talking about the inmates running the prison or trying to please everybody. That's not true. Part of it is leadership, where you need very clear vision. The vision tells you who you are, what business you're in, where you're going, your pictures of the future, and what will drive and guide your journey. I just finished a book with Colleen Barrett of Southwest Airlines. While the airline industry as a whole has lost money, Southwest has made money for thirty-nine straight years. And one of the reasons for this is that the company is so clear about its vision. You ask anybody at the company what business they are in, and they will say, "We are in the customer service business, and we happen to fly airplanes." So their vision is really clear.

Then you can add goals and initiatives. You have to turn the traditional pyramid upside down and work for your people, who eventually work for your customers. This is the servant part of servant leadership, where you empower your people to make decisions so that they don't have to go back to their supervisors. All the research on employee passion says that people want to have a sense of real ownership and real meaning in their work.

FELDMAN: *In your books you discuss situational leadership techniques—leading yourself, individual teams, and organizations. I believe that leadership starts with oneself. Can you give us some examples of how best to lead yourself?*

BLANCHARD: Well, there is this journey in leadership from self, where you get perspective from building trust one-on-one, to building teams where you are developing a sense of community. With the self thing, there are several parts to it. One is to help people learn who they are. We give leaders an instrument that teaches them about their dispositions, and Myers-Briggs, which teaches them about their personalities. We also have them develop leadership points of view, which has them ask the following questions: What do you expect of people? What do they expect of you, and where does that come from? Who are the people in your life who influence your beliefs about leadership? What is your own mission statement? What are your personal values? What are your beliefs about leading and motivating people?

Situational leadership says that there is no one best leadership style—it depends on the situation. So we look at more development levels, like with enthusiastic beginners who need direction. They are all excited about a goal or an opportunity but don't know what they are doing. You need a coaching style that includes tender loving care. Then the employees are at the cautious development level where they know how to do it but they lack the confidence to do it all by themselves. So now you just need a supporting leadership style. And then, finally, employees become self-directed achievers when they have the competency and the commitment, and you can really delegate tasks to them. When people are given goals and objectives in their jobs, we teach them how to analyze their own development levels and to determine what kind of leadership styles they will need for each of their particular goals.

FELDMAN: *What are some tips to create and cultivate leaders within an organization?*

BLANCHARD: Make sure all your people understand that they are leaders. Anytime you try to influence the thinking, beliefs, or behaviors of somebody else, you are engaging in leadership. So one of my employees, who is not a manager, has a chance to influence other people. And once we make that clear to people, then we talk about the different roles. All of us have life-role leadership, but some of us also have organizational leadership. And what you really need to do is get people to understand what it takes to lead and manage other people. If you have people you think have leadership potential, they would have to realize a few main things. First, there's the 80/20 rule. You know, 80 percent of the performance you want from people comes from 20 percent of the things they can do. Once goals are clear, you want to get out of your office, wander around, see if you can catch people doing something right, and give them a one-minute praising because people love to be encouraged.

FELDMAN: *You've mentioned that it's more effective for a manager to start tough and loosen up later. Would you explain that?*

BLANCHARD: Well, we believe that for situational leadership, it is better to provide structure in the beginning—direction and goals and those kinds of things. And if employees look like they are getting better, then you can loosen up. A lot of people will start off really friendly, wanting everybody to get involved in decision making, and then [if] people aren't performing right . . . all of a sudden, they seagull in. They fly in, make a lot of noise, dump on everybody, and fly out. We trained a lot of teachers and we said, you know, in the beginning, maybe you ought not to smile until November. If you are loosey-goosey in the beginning and then you get nonperformance, it is tough to turn it around. Whereas, if you are demanding in the beginning and people respond, then you can loosen up.

"80 PERCENT OF THE PERFORMANCE YOU WANT FROM PEOPLE COMES FROM 20 PERCENT OF THE THINGS THEY CAN DO."

If employees are out of line, if they are beginners, you redirect them back to their goals because maybe, as their manager, you didn't make it clear enough. And you redirect their energy or, if they know better, you give them a one-minute reprimand, tell them what they did wrong, and end with a reaffirmation, which is, "The reason I am upset is that you are one of my best people." Great leaders have the resolve and determination to accomplish goals, but they are also seen as humble. When things go well, they look out the window and give everybody credit, and when things go wrong, they look in the mirror and ask, "What could I have done differently?" For typical self-serving leaders, when things go right, they look in the mirror and pat themselves on the back. When things go poorly, they look out the window to see who they can blame.

FELDMAN: *What's your secret for hiring winners?*

BLANCHARD: One of the things that I do is try to check their backgrounds. Often, people put in references because with all the lawyers you can't really get the truth out of people. So one of my strategies is that I will call people who gave a recommendation for somebody, but I will call them at a time when I am pretty sure they won't be answering the phone. And I will leave a message and say, "We are interviewing so-and-so, and I read your recommendation. If he or she is as good as you say, would you please call me back?"

If they call you back and they go on and on, you can really get some good data on them. And you can ask if there are any other people that you ought to speak to because the best predictor of future behavior is past. So the more you can find out, the better. A lot of times when you read people's resumes it depends on your own insights. You might not have a winner.

FELDMAN: *What are some of the biggest lessons that you may have learned since you published the* One Minute Manager *twenty-eight years ago?*

BLANCHARD: Well, the biggest thing that has changed is that the third secret of the *One Minute Manager* was the one-minute reprimand, which we said was for people who know how to do a job. And then we also told them about redirection, which is when you're working with a potential winner. I think if I would rewrite that book now, I would call the third secret the one-minute redirection. Today, with the speed of the way things are changing, I think everybody out there is a learner.

"AN EFFECTIVE MANAGER NEEDS TO BE CLEAR ABOUT RESPONSIBILITIES AND WHAT WE ARE BEING HELD ACCOUNTABLE FOR..."

FELDMAN: *How do you inspire learning for somebody who thinks, hey, I have gone to college, I have learned all this stuff, I've been in the industry for twenty years, and I don't need to learn anything else? How do you inspire somebody like that? Or do you just get rid of them because they are just not a winner?*

BLANCHARD: Well, I'm not sure you inspire people to learn. I think you're right. I think it is kind of an inner trait that they have. "Share" them with the competition. They are just not going to make it. If people today are not growing and learning, they are going backward.

FELDMAN: *One of the primary foundations of the* One Minute Manager *is One Minute Goal Setting, which can have an incredible impact on both employees and managers. While it's a simple concept, it's more than just about writing down your goals in a minute, isn't it?*

BLANCHARD: Well, in most organizations when you ask people what they do and then ask their boss, all too often you get two different lists. In fact, in some organizations I've worked in, between what I thought my job responsibilities were and what my boss thought they were, any relationship was purely coincidental. And then I would get in trouble for not doing something I didn't even think was my job.

An effective manager needs to be clear about responsibilities and what we are being held accountable for, with each goal recorded on a single page and no more than 250 words long. Anyone should be able pick it up and understand it within a minute, so it needs to be clear and concise. Both the employee and the manager get a copy so everything is clear and so we can both periodically check the progress.

So a manager needs to focus on six basic areas with the One Minute Goal Setting with employees. One, agree on your goals. Two, identify what behaviors need to look like to accomplish the goal. Three, write out each of your goals on a single sheet of paper using fewer than 250 words. Four, read and reread each goal, which requires only a minute or so each time you do it. Five, take a minute every once in a while out of your day to look at your performance. Six, see whether or not your behavior matches your goal.

FELDMAN: *One of the issues that we see in the insurance business is that we don't have enough new talent coming into the industry to replace the ones that are retiring. Many of our readers have sales reps or want them. What are some best practices that we need to know?*

BLANCHARD: Sales is a tough nut to crack. Schools don't teach it, and yet in the real world nothing happens unless you sell something. I hate to use the 80/20 rule again, but you really need to focus on what is the 20 percent that someone needs to do to quickly get on their feet.

"THE BEST SUCCESS STORIES IN SALES ALMOST ALWAYS ARE BYPRODUCTS OF GOING ALONG ON SALES CALLS WITH PEOPLE, WATCHING THEM OPERATE..."

I remember working with IBM years ago, with their salespeople. They had *four* responsibilities: *first* is sales, *second* is service, *third* is administration—did they get the forms filled out and all. And *fourth* was team contribution and mentoring.

The best success stories in sales almost always are byproducts of going along on sales calls with people, watching them operate, role-playing, and, through that, gaining product knowledge and learning to interact with customers. That is the best I've seen. The one-minute leadership and management process is not about what you do to people, it is what you do with them. And so we always find it is really powerful that people will share what they are learning and then see what is going to come out of that.

Final Thoughts

Ken believes in the importance of building trust with your employees to foster a sense of passion and commitment in the workplace. For me, empathy is critical to achieving those goals. If you can relate to the struggles your employees may be going through, then you'll care more about helping them overcome them. Employees and coworkers need to know that you care about them, that you care about their mission, and that you care about the company before they can fully trust you to lead them. No one will want to work for a company whose owner doesn't seem to care very much about them. Even if the company is successful, a founder or executive team that drifts away from the people that work, day in and day out, to keep their company great will eventually doom themselves.

I tell my employees regularly that, outside of their families, I care about them more than any other person in the world. And I mean it. I care about their success, and I view their ability to achieve it as a reflection on my leadership skills. When they come to work, I want them to know two things: one, that they will be able to do their job well; and two, that they will be happy doing it. If my workers aren't happy, then I'm not going to be happy, either. If that correlation diminishes in any way, I know I'm at risk of losing touch with my workers.

It all circles back to company culture. Culture is what defines your company and what drives the people. Do they like coming to work every day? You must create an environment that people like to work in, and that comes down from management.

I realized fairly early on that as a leader, I was being watched all the time and the behaviors employees observed would be replicated. I had to look at the way I carried myself as a bellwether for our culture. If their leader is snarky about the clients, then guess what? The employees are going to feel the same way about clients. If their leader loves and is passionate about their employees and their clients, then the same attitude permeates through the organization.

Ken identifies the importance of goal setting, praising, transparency, humility, and service as key to this leadership philosophy, not just for managers but for all professionals. Everyone in a company should adopt a sense of leadership, from the CEO down to the entry-level employee and freshest of interns. Adopting a sense of leadership doesn't necessarily make them managers, but it does make them responsible for themselves and what goes on around them. Anytime you try to influence the thinking, beliefs, or behavior of someone else, you are engaging in leadership. It is leadership from within, for the ground up, that makes a company truly successful.

Key Takeaways

GOAL SETTING

First, help your employees understand who they are by using an instrument such as Myers-Briggs. This will help you understand what style of leadership they need and what style they exemplify. Then, be clear about what you want from them and how they can achieve it. Ken advises leaders to follow six steps to achieve setting clear, achievable goals:

1. Agree on your goals.
2. Identify what behaviors need to look like to accomplish the goal.
3. Write out each of your goals on a single sheet of paper using fewer than 250 words.
4. Read and reread each goal.

5. Take a minute out of your day every once in a while to look at your performance.

6. Check to make sure your behavior matches your goal.

ONE-MINUTE PRAISING

People must be encouraged regularly. Once goals are set, take time to praise workers who are meeting them. Like Ken said, "80 percent of the performance you want from people comes from 20 percent of the things they can do."

TRANSPARENCY AND TRUST

Employees should feel that you care about and respect them enough to include them in decisions. Treat them as business partners, and don't make decisions that affect their lives behind closed doors.

HUMILITY

Great leaders have the resolve and determination to accomplish goals, but they are also recognized as humble. To quote Ken, "When things go well, they look out the window and give everybody credit, and when things go wrong, they look in the mirror and ask, 'What could I have done differently?'"

CHAPTER 5

CARING IS CONTAGIOUS (AND PROFITABLE)

Harvey Mackay

My introduction to Harvey Mackay came when, at the age of twenty-one, I bought the audio program of his book *Swim with the Sharks without Being Eaten Alive*. It was relatively young at the time and struggling against people twice my age with twice the experience, and I was not always coming out on top.

I was still working for my dad at the time, and while he was a leader with many great ideas and the will to act on them, when it came down to creating a real plan, sustaining the pace, and then providing the required service for the business he sold, well, that was someone else's job. You can probably guess whose shoulders that job fell on, and well, I didn't always feel prepared.

So I bought Harvey's book on a whim. I have to admit that the title of the program appealed to me at the time, as it probably does to many young professionals. It certainly felt like I was being circled by sharks.

I got my money's worth from the purchase, playing the tapes so often that I literally wore them out. They were on repeat for months and I returned to them regularly. For a while, Harvey's voice became the backdrop to my life. At the time, I was convinced that his voice and words would seep in through my ears and permeate me, permanently etching onto my mind.

Needless to say, interviewing Harvey was surreal. Hearing his distinct voice with his soft Minnesota accent sent me back to those days when I was driving around in my little red BMW convertible, commuting to and from my father's business, Harvey's tapes on repeat. A lot has changed in the business world since then, but the fundamentals that Harvey teaches remain the same. You have to believe in what you do, help others, know your clients, live up to what you say (and more), be persistent, and stay consistent.

What impresses me most about Harvey is that he is a true entrepreneur who built an incredibly successful company before he became a best-selling author and speaker. At the tender age of twenty-six, he bought a failing envelope company and subsequently grew it into a $100 million business employing more than six hundred people. Nearly a half-century later, he continues as the chairman. Harvey is not a speaker who lectures about business. He is a successful businessperson who gives lectures.

You can do all the "right things" and still suffer from lackluster sales. That's because simply doing all the right things doesn't guarantee you'll get all the right results. That is, unless you add a dash of the most important ingredient into your sales strategy: humanization.

That's what Harvey Mackay discovered. And that's exactly what he delivers, too. Readers of Harvey's many best-selling books, such as *Swim with The Sharks without Being Eaten Alive*, along with followers of his widely syndicated newspaper column, know that Harvey tested and proved his ideas within his own company first. A small, failing envelope company when he bought it, Mackay Mitchell Envelope Company has become one of the nation's major envelope manufacturers, producing twenty-five million envelopes a day. He drives his company with the motto: Do what you love, love what you do, and deliver more than you promise. How did he do it? He learned the keys to really successful networking—not just working on a good "How-do-you-do?" but actually becoming indispensable to others. And he is generous with his wisdom, offering tools such as the Mackay 66, a list of the essential things salespeople should know about their prospects and clients. In my interview with Harvey, he talks about this and other insights.

A Conversation with Harvey Mackay

FELDMAN: *Networking is one of the keys for your success. What tips can you give advisors and agents to network more effectively?*

MACKAY: There's only one philosophy that any insurance agent, or any human being, should follow in order to be an effective networker and that is as follows: Every time that you meet a new person, and you extend your hand—"Hi, my name's Harvey Mackay"—immediately your brain bank should say, "What can I do for this person?" Now, that's not an earth-shattering philosophy; a lot of people have been espousing that for years. Not many people practice it, but many do espouse it. Then, the key is to expect nothing in return. Once you've achieved that as a way of life, the world is yours. That's what I teach my children. That's what I practice every single day. It is the cornerstone of my whole philosophy and how I run my company.

FELDMAN: *How important is "knowing thy" customer, and what are some strategies from the Mackay 66, which you feature in* Swim with the Sharks without Being Eaten Alive?

MACKAY: That was a defining moment in my life, when at age twenty-one I came up with sixty-six questions that I wanted to know about three hundred purchasing managers, the envelope buyers. The questions were what I wanted to know from Pillsbury, General Mills, 3M, Honeywell, all of these people. But obviously, I wanted to know about that particular person. I wanted to know about their spouse, their family, their interests, whether they were politically active, and how they thought things were going in the country, which is so very important. I wanted to know what their passion was, what turned them on. I wanted to know what kind of activities they like. Are they hikers, bikers? Are they golfers, tennis players? That would give me a feel, a touch, and a pulse of the people.

Not only do we use "the 66" for all of our customers, but we also use it for anybody that comes through our front door. I want the best envelope machines in the country. I want the best paper suppliers in the country. I want the best ink suppliers, the best box suppliers. So anyone who comes through my door is someone who we want to build a long-term relationship with. And we do it with the sixty-six question customer profile, which is what I call it.

What's critical is once you know all that, it means zero unless you perform. You have to perform first and then build the relationship.

But here's a little vignette I tell as a cautionary note, the story about the meticulous spender who had a little black book. He kept track of every single penny, nickel, dime, quarter, dollar he spent: the chewing gum at the airport, newspapers, magazines. Every time he spent anything, he wrote it down. There's only one problem—he never stopped to add it up. And so what we find in sales forces and insurance agents is they keep track but they don't really understand the fundamental concept.

FELDMAN: *How do you define the fundamental concept and personally engage in using it?*

MACKAY: It's to humanize your selling strategy. So what I used to do every Sunday, for the first twenty-five years of my selling career, was go through my three hundred accounts and read the 66. I would put it into my brain bank and figure out creative ways to act on that information. Knowledge does not become power until it's used. Ideas without action are worthless. As an example, we now have three thousand accounts with our thirty-person sales force. And I would say that virtually all of our salespeople know when their buyer's birthday is. Well, you wouldn't believe how much business we write on a buyer's birthday. We try to see them in person and bring them a very creative gift. We're not buying their business; we just know what their passion is and we find them the little things. So Paul, let's just say you're my client or prospect and you're a golfer, and I just happen to know Arnold Palmer is your hero. Well, once I know that, I would find out when Palmer's writing a book, and I would buy that book immediately. Then I'd get his address and FedEx it to him with a very clever letter saying: Paul is one of my big accounts and he loves you and respects you. Can you just write in there, "Dear Paul, give Harvey all your business." I walk in on your birthday. I give you that book. That's not buying your business, that's just being creative.

What I learned at age twenty-one is what I want to find out about every single person I call on, what their passion is, what turns them on, what they're interested in. If you're an insurance agent, you can't walk in and talk business 100 percent of the time. According to studies, it's about 65/35: 65 percent is social and 35 percent is business. So I found a company that manufactures twenty thousand kinds of sports memorabilia. You name me any athlete in the United States and I can get you the hockey stick, bowling ball, jersey, baseball, basketball, all signed, and that's what I do.

I'm trying to always think, it doesn't matter if I'm selling envelopes and I'm calling on General Mills or Medtronic. When I call on that buyer, what can I do for them? I'm not just thinking about them and their family. I'm thinking about what I can do for their company, which will put that purchasing manager in line for maybe even a raise.

FELDMAN: *How does a manager get salespeople to implement the Mackay 66?*

MACKAY: Well, number one, people will no longer be working for me if they don't practice that philosophy. They have to understand that this is how we sell, that this is how we become differentiators and humanize our selling strategy. I am constantly looking at our charts, and if I see all of a sudden an account is going way down and I see a trend, I call the salesperson into my office and I tell him or her, "Bring your 66 with you." And they might explain that there's a new buyer there and I'll ask, "Well, what do you know about them?" If they don't know a lot and the 66 isn't basically filled in, then, depending on how long they've been there, that account is no longer theirs.

So they have to buy into that strategy. First of all, it's fun. It's really fun to probe and to be inquisitive. If you don't have a deep-down, burning desire to find out about your buyers or the people you're doing business with, then you surely don't belong in the selling business. I say caring is contagious, help spread it around. If I'm calling on you and it happens your wife or child is very sick, I'll have access to fabulous doctors because that's part of the thing I'm practicing. We're teaching all of our people to have many contacts and build their networks so that they can pass on to the people all these different assets that they've got in their network.

So they have to believe in the 66. I haven't seen anything else in the last fifty years that supplants getting to know your customer.

"WE ARE JUDGED BY WHAT WE FINISH, NOT BY WHAT WE START."

FELDMAN: *Hiring is one of the hardest things for any business owner. Your company, on the other hand, has a long success of hiring. What is your secret?*

MACKAY: If you're going to build an insurance agency or anything, the hiring is very important. I've hired every single person myself, and we've got close to six hundred on the payroll. I even hired the switchboard operators. I hired the truck drivers too up to about ten years ago. Now, I just hire all the key people. And what I call "key" is our sales force, our HR people, BP manufacturing, and so forth. But that all starts with my hiring process.

You cannot build a business with a revolving door. And therefore you can't be wrong. You've gotta be right. And if you're right 80 percent of the time, you're genius level. Frankly, I am almost above that figure. I do something extraordinarily controversial and I don't expect a lot of companies to do this, but it works for me.

I run all of our candidates through an industrial psychologist, which is much more inexpensive than the mistake of a bad hire. They don't make the decision for you, but if you have concerns, they'll find out about them. Candidates are also run through a series of interviews: with HR, key executives, and even close friends of mine whom I trust explicitly.

"FAILURE IS NO MORE FATAL THAN SUCCESS IS PERMANENT."

In fifty years, I never hired a person without going to their home. (If married) I'll interview the spouse and even their children. That gives me an arrow in my quiver on core values, on character, on goals, on dreams, on aspirations, and on education. It tells me a lot. I usually let the spouse know that this is the single biggest decision I'm going to make the whole year. And even though we have six hundred people, I'm only hiring two salesmen this year. Therefore, I want to let you know that if we're wrong, we're still going to be in business but it's going be catastrophic for you. So I want you to know what my company stands for and what our philosophy is.

FELDMAN: *What do you look for in a salesperson that's different than what you'd look for in another type of position? What are some key traits, characteristics?*

MACKAY: The acid test of hiring is somewhere between the ten- and fifteen-minute mark of the interview, I will say the following to myself,

"How would I feel if Paul were working for my competitor?" And if I'm not worried, that's the end of the interview.

Next, the most important word in the English language—if you're going to be a salesman, especially an insurance salesman—is trust. Without trust, you don't have a marriage. You don't have a boss-to-sales-manager relationship, you can't become an entrepreneur, you can't have people working for you, you can't have good friends, you can't have anything without trust.

Then there are three things that I look for. Number one is a hungry fighter. Number two is a hungry fighter. And number three is a hungry fighter. That is what they unequivocally, absolutely, have to be.

They also have to be a self-starter. We call it TGIM at Mackay Envelope—Thank God It's Monday. We've got hundreds and hundreds and hundreds of people that can't wait to get to work on Monday. How do I know that? I meet with all of our people, every one of them, in the hundreds. And I have a Mackay 66 on all our employees.

So if someone from the printing department comes in, I know whether he's been married, how many kids he has, what turns him on, when his kid's graduating. If I have to reprimand him, I will and then say, "Oh, incidentally, I see John just graduated from high school . . ."

FELDMAN: *You say people buy likability, but is there a way to improve your likability?*

MACKAY: Well, surely. People buy from other people because of chemistry, likability, and people skills. And, again, it's meaningless if you don't perform. But if you perform and then also do these other things, you won't lose the business. How can you become more likeable? You have to be interesting. You have to know what's going on in the world. You have to know what's going on in your community. You have to know what's going on in their life, to be as knowledgeable as you can. You have to be a voracious reader and know about what's going on in the country and the world and in literature so that you can be quoting all kinds of things.

FELDMAN: *You're famous for your time-saving tips. What are some key ones?*

MACKAY: I've never started a meeting without holding up my watch and saying, "We have no competitors except this." And I dangle my watch. I say, "We all start out life with one thing in common. We all have the same amount of time. Now it's just a matter of what we do with it." And so they understand time immediately. Also for time management, I find out the habits of all of my buyers. And we'd call on some printing plants on Saturday. Some worked the graveyard shift; some worked in the evening. You have to know when you can hit those people. And if you're a good planner, you can get in way more calls by starting at 7:45 a.m., or if someone's in their office at 7:30 and you're right there bringing them the newspaper and coffee or whatever. And you're also there at 6 p.m. because you know they work late. So the time-management habits of all of your customers are important. I always keep copious notes on the 66. If I take you to lunch, when I get back in my car, I will not start my engine. I'll take out my BlackBerry and dictate. I'll say he's this, he's this, he's this. His dream is to go to Augusta, just got back from Belgium . . . And I'll dictate all 66 items or as many as I got. Then I have it transcribed.

Now that is time management. I never, ever, make a call on anyone without dictating, after the meeting's over with, everything that we discussed, everything that I learned about them, so that I can build on that particular person. Now when I go see him again, I'll just get that file out and I'm way more effective.

FELDMAN: *You also stress community involvement and volunteerism.*

MACKAY: You can't get dealt a straight flush unless you're in the game. Insurance people, they have to be out there. What do I mean by out there? Yes, you join a country club. But I mean you have to still go out there and be a good guy and participate. See, I didn't know this and my father sat me down as soon as I graduated college and said, "About a fourth to a third of your life is going to be in volunteerism." I didn't even have a job. I just spent four years in school and he's telling me that I'm going to be a volunteer the rest of my life. So I did wind up on twenty boards and was president of many of those boards. But here's what happens. You follow your passion and let's say you join the United Way or Salvation Army, that's what you love, those are two of my favorites. And every nonprofit over the past two, three, four years, has been in deep trouble.

They have their back to the wall and they have to raise money. So if you're a volunteer and now you raise money, what does that mean? You're going to knock on doors, you're going to make phone calls. You're going to get a lot of nos and learn to handle rejection and become a better speaker because you're selling. You become a better communicator, a better leader, a better sales manager.

When I was twenty-two, twenty-three years old and the Minnesota State Cancer Chairman, I had twenty-five people working for me. I became a leader and a speaker, I had to go around to twelve clinics and twelve small towns in Minnesota and put on a cancer clinic. That's probably the biggest single thing that helped me become a speaker.

FELDMAN: *In your decades of experience, have you noticed fundamental themes that all people should live by and understand?*

MACKAY: The biggest room in the world is the room for improvement. Regardless of your God-given potential or talent, you will be able to improve at whatever you intend to do. A leader or successful salesperson and entrepreneur must understand that they have strengths and weaknesses and, by not recognizing those weaknesses, arrogance can set in. So it's imperative that each human being understands what their strong suit is and what their weaknesses are.

"THE SINGLE CHARACTERISTIC SHARED BY ALL THE TRULY SUCCESSFUL PEOPLE I'VE MET OVER A LIFETIME IS THE ABILITY TO CREATE AND NURTURE A NETWORK OF CONTACTS."

You can't do it all by yourself. Even the Lone Ranger had Tonto. There's no substitute for teamwork, especially in today's marketplace when the world is changing so rapidly. You have to have advisors, counselors, and people you can bounce your ideas off of. And I call that a kitchen cabinet. Every person should have a kitchen cabinet—three, four, five people who care about him or her.

One final thing that must be understood is that you don't go to school once for a lifetime. You're in school all of your life. I'd hate to have major surgery from a doctor who graduated from medical school twenty years ago and didn't keep up with the modern-day medical technology. So, in short, if you think education is expensive, try ignorance.

Final Thoughts

My interviews with Harvey ran for two hours on two separate occasions. We spent considerable time together, and one thing (among many) I can vouch for is this: Harvey is clearly a man who walks the talk. Not only did we have an amazing conversation, but he then followed up with every promise he made and more. Within days of our conversation, he had sent me an autographed set of all of his books, a copy of two articles he mentioned in the interview, and a handwritten thank-you note, which has become a lost art these days.

Learning how to be special, as a differentiator in people's lives, is the key to not only good sales but also to a good life. If you ask me, no one embodies that truth more than the legendary Harvey Mackay.

A few days after we published the second part of this interview—in which we discuss his book, *MBA of Sales*—I was floored when I received an unforgettable five-page thank-you letter. It was simple, sincere, and memorable, which is exactly how you want to be to both customers and other business professionals.

Key Takeaways

According to Harvey, **networking** requires a selfless mind-set. As soon as you meet someone, ask yourself how you can benefit that person. Continue your relationship with the same sentiment, and do it without expecting anything in return.

Know people intimately. Learn their Mackay 66 and use the sum of the answers to find creative ways to reach and please them. If nothing else, know their passions. When interacting, talk 65 percent personal and 35 percent business. With employees in particular, consider meeting their families before hiring them. And make use of positive things you know are happening in their personal lives to include any unpleasant conversations, such as reprimands.

PART II: SALES

CHAPTER 6
THE LAW OF SALES SUCCESS

Brian Tracy

T

o some, "sales" is something of a dirty word that evokes images of a desperate Willy Loman or the unscrupulous salesmen of *Glengarry Glen Ross* and other Hollywood distortions. In truth, we are all in sales to some degree, in both our professional and personal lives. A husband sells his wife on his "need" for a new car; kids sell their parents on the alleged "value" of the newest video game console; leaders sell their vision to their employees; and employees sell their managers on why they deserve a raise. But persuasion is not the same thing as manipulation. Unlike manipulation, persuasion is often principled and founded in facts and reality. *One need not distort to convince.*

Sales is an art of persuasion, not manipulation. I always say that it's simply a transfer of emotion from one person to another. When done successfully, you create happiness in your prospect by solving their problem. Sometimes that means you have to inform them that there is a problem, while other times you have to help them find solutions to the problems they already have.

Whether you are someone just starting out in sales or a seasoned salesperson determined to master your profession, a good place to start learning is with author and consultant Brian Tracy. He has written more than forty-five books and has put out the all-time highest-selling audio program about doing sales, *The Psychology of Selling*, which I highly recommend. According to Brian, "Your ability to sell others on your ideas will determine your success in your life and career as much as any other factor." He also believes that every single person in the top 10 percent today, a destination that should be one of your goals, started out in the bottom 10 percent. In other words, every master was once a disaster.

"Sales" is the process by which our economy operates, yet many people don't think of themselves as natural salespeople. The truth, though, is that sales is a learnable skill that everyone should master.

How do you master sales? Brian says it's all about learning, mentoring, practicing, and consistently measuring and rating your sales performance.

In my own life, I was fortunate that sales came somewhat naturally to me, but I still had a lot to learn. I liked the face-to-face, belly-to-belly style of selling since my days spent peddling CDs, video games, cigarettes, radar detectors, and whatever else my high school classmates were into at the time. The personal connection you can make that way helped me learn how to influence people, how to take them in a direction they might not have imagined before they were shown the rewards.

That same satisfaction and thrill I got from selling has stayed with me ever since, but what's changed is the pride I take in what we can provide for our clients. Our clients pay us a fraction of the money they make from our service. That's the kind of cost–benefit ratio that powers growth because it's a symbiotic relationship that enables long-term relationships and boxes out competitors. When it comes to sales, I'm very confident in what I do because I know exactly what I am going to deliver.

I've never used a sales strategy that allowed me to take somebody's money if I knew I couldn't do a service. If I couldn't follow through, I didn't do it. Anyone can sell anything to anyone anywhere because it's easy to make promises. What's not easy is delivering those promises. For a sales strategy to be sustainable, I learned to underpromise and overdeliver. And the only way to do that is to care about your clients, sometimes more than they care about themselves.

When I spoke to Brian, he said that in order to be successful at sales and reach the top 10 percent, you have to be a "sales athlete." As with professional athletes in sports, sales athletes must engage in extensive training, studying, and practice to stay competitive and remain at the top of their game. The struggle continues even once you reach a world-class level. When Tiger Woods tied for fortieth place at the 2012 Masters, he was asked what happened. He replied, "What's frustrating is I know what to do and I just don't do it. I fall back into the same old patterns again and I just need to do more reps." Tiger is still struggling to get back to the top of his game. It takes a lot of hard work to get to the top, and when you arrive, the struggle continues. Your competition is working to get there, too. Staying on top means staying competitive, forever and always.

My interview with Brian was particularly meaningful for me because it was the first one he gave after one of the greatest tribulations of his life—his battle with throat cancer. It took marshalling all of his skills and strengths to defeat the disease, but he learned much from the process that is applicable to all struggles. That he has chosen to share that battle with you and me is testament to his mission to always help others. This generosity only deepened my appreciation for Brian's invaluable contribution to the world.

If you're looking for time-tested strategies for success or just some solid, straight-up wisdom, you can't do much better than talking to Brian. Not only does his no-nonsense advice help foster a better understanding of how to sell, but his reassuring style also invites listeners and readers into his world of calm confidence. That style is a big reason why the audio series of *The Psychology of Selling* is reportedly the best-selling audio program on sales in history and why his consultation for more than a thousand companies has seen him speak to more than four million people in four thousand speeches and seminars.

In this conversation, Brian discusses the how-tos of improving both your business and your life. He also tells the legendary Ben Feldman (no relation) story as only he can.

A Conversation with Brian Tracy

FELDMAN: *What are some of your key strategies for effective time management?*

TRACY: The first thing to understand is that if you do not deliberately manage your time, your time will get out of control. The default setting on the human being, especially in sales, is underachievement and failure. If you want to break that, you've really got to become very good at time management.

When I first started studying time management, I was astonished. I thought it was sort of like a peripheral thing that you did in the course of your lifetime. What I found later was that it's the most important thing you do in life. Your time management largely determines your success. So I just began to study it. And as you begin to study it—

surprise, surprise—you get better at it. If you look at the people in the top 20 percent, there are no exceptions. They all use their time better. And what I say is that when we start off in life, we start off with lots of time and no money. And over the course of your working lifetime, if you use your time well, you end up with a lot of money and less time. The worst of all is to use up all your time and end up broke after twenty or thirty years of working, which unfortunately is too common.

There are three critical things in time management. Number one, plan your time in advance. And the way you do that, based on enormous research, is you make a list of everything you have to do at the beginning of each day—preferably the night before so that your mind can work on it overnight. Number two, you set priorities on your list and you pick the most important things that you have to do. If you could only do one thing the following day, what would it be? And then number three is, in the morning, you start on your most important task and you stay with it until it's done. If you do that, you're going to have a fabulous life. You're going to accomplish two, three, five, even ten times as much as other people. You're going to be wealthy and successful. You're going to have a tremendous sense of personal accomplishment. You'll have high self-esteem and self-confidence. You're going to be respected by everybody around you. And if you don't, you're not. It's black and white.

One of the great things I've found is that nature is neutral. Nature doesn't care where you're coming from and what you started with. Your education or background or family, or anything else, doesn't matter. If you do what other successful people do, you get the same results. And if you don't, you don't. Nature is neutral.

FELDMAN: *That's profound.*

TRACY: Absolutely, it's so important to understand that. Some of the most successful people in financial services of all kinds are people who started with absolutely nothing and struggled for a long time before they became successful.

FELDMAN: *Can you explain your law of sales?*

TRACY: The first law is that nothing happens in sales until the sale takes place. We're really coming back to time management. The key to time management—an expert told me this and I never forgot it—is managing the sequence of events. In other words, managing what you do first, what you do second, and what you do not do at all. Time management means that you have so many things to do and you choose the order. And, in the choice of the order, you determine your entire life. So when we say nothing happens until the sale takes place, then what salespeople need to do is spend 80 percent of their time selling.

Now there's a law of three that I keep. And it seems to be true for every single occupation. The law of three says that there are three things that you do in the course of a day, whatever your job is, that account for 90 percent of your income. If you're in management, there are three. If you're a cardio physician, there are three. If you're a mechanic, there are three. If you're a business owner, there are three. It varies depending upon your occupation, but there are only three. The way that you determine what your three are, and I've done this with thousands of people in my seminars, is by making a list of everything you do in the course of the day. And then ask yourself if you could only do one thing on this list, all day long, which one activity would contribute the most to your income? And that will pop out at you. And then you ask the question again. If you could only do two things all day long, which would be number two? And then if you could only do three things all day long, which would be number three? I have done this now for over twelve years. It works 100 percent of the time. Then I say there is always one key task and two support tasks. In selling, we know what they are. They are prospecting, presenting, and closing. Those are the three.

There are many other sales activities. There's getting organized and planning and sending out follow-up letters and all kinds of things. But the three that are most important, upon which everything else is determined, are prospecting, presenting, and closing. Prospecting is the point of the spear. It's talking to more people. Presenting is making sure that your presentation is persuasive, effective, customer focused, customer-centric. And then closing—getting the customer to make a decision, sign the contract, and give you a check. Those are the three.

If you're having problems in selling, give yourself a grade of one to ten in each of those three. And you'll know instantly what your big problem is and what is determining your income today. And what you realize is that these are learnable skills. Every single person who is good at sales was once poor. So what you do is simply settle down and get really, really good on the most important skill that can help you the most. And whether that takes you a week or a month or a year, you put your head down and become really, really good at the one skill that is determining your income. And whenever people do that, they're absolutely astonished. They go from rags to riches in as little as a year.

FELDMAN: *One of my favorite approaches that you have is to reverse-engineer your presentation. Can you tell us a little bit more about that?*

TRACY: Reverse-engineering is when you start with the end in mind. And in selling, the end is when the client accepts your recommendation, signs the contract, and gives you a check. So, you work back to the beginning. What has to happen from the very beginning in order for you to achieve that at the end?

"EVERY SINGLE PERSON WHO IS GOOD AT SALES WAS ONCE POOR."

One of the first things you have to do is to prospect and talk to the right people. Who is the ideal client for me as an insurance professional? Who is the ideal client who will buy from me, will buy again, will recommend their friends, and will be happy with my services? Who needs it? We start to ask that question.

People say, oh, everybody needs insurance, or anybody that's got money or anybody that's got extra income. Well, that's fine if you have no future. But you really have to sit down and think about it.

I'll give you an example. A good friend of mine has been in the Top of the Table starting about three years after he began in insurance and he's now a multimillionaire. He started off in life insurance and they told him go call on doctors, lawyers, architects, engineers, people with high income. Those are the best people to buy insurance. So he went out, and can you guess what he found? He found that every insurance agent within five hundred miles was calling on all those people. So he couldn't even get appointments, because those people were just being inundated by insurance professionals trying to get appointments with people who had money.

So he backed up and he said, "How do I get to see these people? Well, I need to have a really good understanding of their situation." So he picked the medical profession and focused on doctors. And then he started to do research. How do they earn money? What does it cost them to run their practice? What kind of insurance do they need? And he began to interview doctors. As he interviewed doctors, he wrote articles, which he then published in journals that doctors read on the essential requirements for financial planning for medical professionals. Well, eventually, they began to invite him to give talks to local chapters on how doctors could organize their lives so that they could end up financially independent. And he would talk about the pitfalls, the things they had to consider, and the various alternatives they had. And afterward, can you guess what happened? People would say, "Well, could you come and see me? A lot of what you said made sense to me."

Soon he was being invited to address national conventions on financial planning for medical professionals. And he mastered the skill of selling to medical professionals. Pretty soon, he became the go-to person. People began to recommend him and give referrals. And the more doctors he sold to, the more doctors would recommend him. So he had incredible credibility, social proof, testimonials, and went on to hit the Million Dollar Round Table mark in his third year.

FELDMAN: *Closing is often the most painful part of the sales presentation, which is interesting because when it's done right, you don't even need to close. What can you tell those in sales who struggle with closing?*

TRACY: If your product or service is very closely aligned with what your clients want and need and are willing to pay for, then they'll be ready to buy at the end. They still need to be asked, but they'll be ready to buy. Closing should be low pressure or no pressure at all. You're just asking the customer to confirm everything you've talked about up to that point. So closing could be as simple as saying, "Does this make sense to you so far?" If the prospect says yes, you say, "Well let's get started right away." Real simple. It's not a technique where you twist the customer's arm up behind their back.

FELDMAN: *So how do you draw them in from the beginning?*

TRACY: Focus on the customer's needs, and there are two very simple ways to do that. Identify the pain that the customer has, the problems that arise because of lack of being properly insured, and then the benefit, the peace of mind, the financial stability, the provision for your family. Then you use examples of people who accepted your advice and this is what happened or people who decided not to and this is what happened to them. A positive example and negative example— both are good. And they don't have to be your examples. They can be examples from someone else.

I remember when I bought my first million-dollar policy from the gentleman I was talking about earlier. Because I was going back and forth, he told me a story of a business owner who had decided not to insure. And when the business owner died, after they had taken all the taxes and paid off all the bills and everything else, his wife, who thought he would be worth more than a million dollars, was destitute within three years and had to move in with the couple's adult children. Was that what he wanted? I never heard the story before, but it was a real eye-opener for me. That's exactly why I bought the insurance and I continually insure myself for millions of dollars.

"THERE ARE TWO VERY SIMPLE WAYS TO FOCUS ON THE CUSTOMER'S NEEDS. IDENTIFY THE PAIN THAT THE CUSTOMER HAS... AND THEN THE BENEFIT, THE PEACE OF MIND, THE FINANCIAL STABILITY, THE PROVISION FOR YOUR FAMILY."

Later I spoke to another insurance agent on the other side of the country and he started telling me the same story. It turned out it was a story about a businessman in Florida. And the same story—the identical story—had been circulated throughout the insurance industry and all the estate planners all use the same story, nationwide.

FELDMAN: *One of the most effective closing techniques that I have come across is the one that you call "The Instant Reverse-Close." It is almost magical because it instantly changes the state of your prospect's mind unlike anything I have ever seen. Can you explain it for readers?*

TRACY: When a person says, "I'm not interested," you immediately say, "That's exactly why I'm calling on you. I didn't think you'd be interested. Most of my very best clients were not interested when I first called on them, but now they recommend me to their friends." What that does is it just simply gets their attention, by taking their best objection and telling them, "That is exactly why you should do." That's just one opportunity for an instant reverse-close. Another thing that I used to say when I was selling financial services is, "I want you to know that I am not here to sell you anything. Please relax. All I want to do is ask you a couple of questions and see if I can't help you achieve some of your goals in a cost-effective way. Then we'll do everything possible to help you achieve those goals. Would that be all right?"

Then you take control of the questioning process. The questions start from the general and they go to the particular. The first question is very easy to answer. The second question is fairly easy. The third is still easy. And with the fourth question you start to focus on critical things. The questions are progressively more difficult, so it's like a narrowing funnel.

Your questions must be thought through in advance. I design every sales presentation around seven questions. You could have nine or ten, but seven seems to be the ideal, from the most general to the most particular.

FELDMAN: *You have referenced and worked directly with an industry legend, Ben Feldman, many times in your work, and I know you've learned some invaluable lessons from him.*

TRACY: Yes, I used to work with him many years ago. Ben Feldman, you know, was the *Guinness Book of World Records* top insurance salesman in history. He made $15 million a year selling policies one-on-one, head-to-head, knee-to-knee, one person at a time. And he never, never worked more than fifty miles away from East Liverpool,

Ohio, which is the little town he settled in when he was twenty years old.

He was making $13 million to $15 million a year and he had a staff of thirty-five people that just processed the business he wrote. And he did all his business with small-businesspeople within driving distance of his home because he promised his wife and his family he'd always be home for dinner and he always was. He was the master of the incisive question. And one of my favorite questions from Ben was one he'd use when he called on a business owner and they would say, "I'm not interested, I don't want it. I can't afford it. I'm not going to bet against myself. I think life insurance is a gamble. It's a waste of money," and all the objections that people give. And he'd say, "Well, that's fine. I appreciate your opinion very much and thank you very much for giving me a little bit of time. But I'm going to ask you just one question before I go. Will your widow be able to dress as well as your wife?" And the businessman would stop like he'd been slapped in the face. He'd say, "What do you mean?"

Ben would reply, "Well, here are the statistics. Within about three years and four months, your wife will be destitute. She'll never again enjoy the standard of living you're providing for her now if you're not properly insured." The guy would say, "Could you come in and explain that to me a little bit more?" And Ben would walk out of there with large checks. He never mentioned his company. He never mentioned the details. Most people bought the insurance from him without even knowing what company he worked for, because it didn't even matter. All that mattered was that if you sign this, then when we get the medical tests through, you will have provided 100 percent for your wife and for your family. Isn't that the most important thing? Isn't that what you're working for in the first place? That guy went on and made $15 million a year—and this is twenty, thirty years ago—as a life insurance salesman.

Ben was not handsome, dashing, or articulate. He was just very good at what he did. He studied life insurance two hours a night, five to seven nights a week. He never stopped studying. He would come home and have dinner between 6 and 8 p.m. Then, from 8 to 10 p.m., he'd go into his little office and he would study life insurance, sales, marketing, actuarial tables, and history, and read every magazine and every book on the subject. He studied two hours a day for his entire career.

And I sometimes mention that to people because I've spoken with most of the life insurance companies in America and throughout the world. I say, "Here's the highest-paid, most successful life insurance professional of his generation—really, of almost all generations. And at the peak of his game, he was still studying two hours a day. Now, how many hours a day are you studying? You, who are struggling and trying to get up there, how many hours are you studying?" And the whole audience looks down and looks away because they think that they're so damn smart, they don't have to study. They're so damn smart, they're just going to go out there and they're going to find people and wing it, when the smartest and highest-paid people in this industry worldwide never stopped studying.

FELDMAN: *I'm a firm believer in continuing my own education, yet so many people say that they just don't have the time for it. I saw a study recently that said the average American in one day watches more than four hours of TV, spends about two hours and forty-five minutes driving,* *listening to the radio about 70 percent of that time, and spends an hour on Facebook. How can people believe that they don't have the time to learn?*

TRACY: You know, I worked it out. There are 168 hours in a week. Most highly paid people work about fifty to sixty hours a week. So if you take fifty hours for work, that's 118 left over. Take eight hours a day for sleeping, and you've got sixty-two hours left. Now let's say you take two hours a day for traveling, that's fourteen hours. All right, now we're down to forty-eight hours. Let's say you eat two hours a day. Okay, now we're down to thirty-four hours. So all you do is you take two hours a day of that, that's fourteen. That gives you twenty hours to watch television all week long.

And the interesting thing is the investment of those fourteen hours will pay itself back five, ten, fifteen, twenty times in additional income over the course of your lifetime. And all you have to do is read a little bit in the morning, listen to educational audio programs as you travel around, and read a little bit in the evenings and on the weekend. Don't try to do it all at once. Go to courses and seminars whenever you have a chance. Meet with other professional people and ask for their advice. What books do they recommend? What techniques and methods have been helpful for them? Just make it so you invest two hours a day in yourself throughout your career.

That will absolutely guarantee that you're going to be a huge success, going to be in the top 10 percent of the highest paid people in your field. You'll live in a beautiful house, drive a beautiful car, have a bank account full of money, and be one of the most respected people in your community. And there are virtually no exceptions to that. The automatic default setting is what? Five hours and fifteen minutes of television a day. That's the average adult in North America: read very seldom, drive around listening to the radio, and wonder why life doesn't get better.

FELDMAN: *Jim Rohn said it best when he said, "Formal education will make you a living; self-education will make you a fortune." You have to be a self-learner in today's world.*

TRACY: You have to be what I call a sales athlete. You could take an athlete, and if an athlete decided not to work out, how long would that person be competitive? You could be in the Olympic Games and win a medal. And if you decide not to work out for a year and then go back into sports, you'll be years behind your competitors who were working out the whole time. People don't realize that, as a sales athlete, you work with your mind. And as a sales athlete, working out your mental fitness means working out with your mind, getting better and better at what you do, smarter and smarter, and more focused.

Final Thoughts

Brian's interview helped to validate a tough choice I'd had to make in my own sales team. Some months after Brian and I spoke, I had to let go a sales manager with thirty years of experience, and the decision still weighed on my mind at the time. No good leader likes to fire people, as it can often reflect poor leadership if workers are not successful under your command. The sales manager in question closed sales, but he never hit his goals. That's not what an employer wants to see, of course, but it wasn't why I let him go. The reason he no longer works for me is because he did not engage in self-improvement and therefore experienced no professional growth. He was complacent with his performance—so much so that if I approached him about underperformance, he was quick with excuses and blame. There was always a scapegoat: the support team, the global economy, the local market, always something or someone to blame, but never himself.

When I tried to share some of my favorite sales books with him, he waved them away. He claimed to know everything in them without even glancing at the books. That was when I knew things weren't going to work out. Now that he no longer works for me, he is a competitor. But he can't keep up with an ever-improving me, not without improving himself.

Being the best means constantly training, learning, and improving. The world gives most of us about the same amount of time, but it is up to the individual to make the most of that time.

Brian says that sales is really nothing more than aligning with a prospect and redirecting. Align and redirect. You get the trust, and then you redirect them. It sounds deceivingly simple, I know, but Brian has plenty of takeaways to help make that phenomenon much easier.

Key Takeaways

SELF-IMPROVEMENT

Always keep learning more about what you think you already know. People change, technology changes, and there will always be new and improved ways of doing things. You have to evolve your systems and techniques for maximum efficiency.

TIME MANAGEMENT

A recurring theme among experts is that managing your time effectively is critical to success, no matter what the objective may be. The top 20 percent of business professionals all use their time better than everyone else, and the key to time management is how you sequence tasks. Brian advises using a three-step plan to achieve better time management:

1. Make a list of everything you have to do at the beginning of each day—preferably the night before so that your mind can work on it overnight.
2. Set priorities on your list by asking, "If I can only do one thing the following day, what will it be?"
3. In the morning, start on your most important task and stay with it until it's done.

Closing should be easy. Utilize **market knowledge** to know the needs of your customer base inside and out. Your clients shouldn't view you as a salesperson; they should view you as someone with expert knowledge of your industry who happens to have solutions to their problems for sale. From the very beginning, focus on their needs. As Brian says, "If your product or service is very closely aligned with what your clients want and need and are willing to pay for, then they'll be ready to buy at the end." At the end, all you'll have to do is say, "Does everything make sense so far?" and as they say yes, you've essentially won your close.

CHAPTER 7
THE ULTIMATE INSURANCE SALES MACHINE

Chet Holmes

Imagine owning a business that practically runs itself, where prospects seek you out, where your marketing and your presentations are highly effective and systematic, and with a system that processed every piece of business with minimal glitches. If you have Sirius/XM or AM radio, then you have probably heard Chet Holmes and his former business partner, Anthony Robbins, promoting their Business Mastery and the Ultimate Sales Machine products that tell you exactly how to do just that.

What insurance agent or financial advisor wouldn't want to possess the Ultimate Sales Machine? According to Chet, any insurance producer can apply four strategies immediately to make his or her business a sales machine: target small, prepare early, hire for attitude, and commit to mastery.

Becoming a master salesperson was Chet's big promise in his book *The Ultimate Sales Machine*, and I have to say that this book (and system) lived up to the hype. Chet's book was one of the most influential books I've ever read. Since its publication in 2008, I have given scores of copies of *The Ultimate Sales Machine* to colleagues and employees, and I continue to recommend it to this day.

Being a black belt, Chet stressed the importance of mastery, systems, and targeting ideal clients with laser-like precision. When asked his secret to becoming a karate master, he says, "It's not doing four thousand karate moves. There aren't four thousand karate moves. It's doing twelve moves four thousand times each. That's what makes a master."

This is as true for sales, and all business, as it is for the martial arts. According to Chet, professionals are better positioned for success by mastering a few skills rather than dabbling in everything.

I am thankful to have had the opportunity to interview Chet before his untimely passing at age fifty-five following his battle with leukemia. During his life, Chet inspired hundreds of thousands of business owners and entrepreneurs to become "masters" of their trade.

In this interview, I talk with Chet about his four proven strategies, methods that can help producers double their sales in twelve months.

A Conversation with Chet Holmes

FELDMAN: *What is the first thing you tell a producer to do to boost sales?*

HOLMES: One of the things that insurance agents don't do very well is target effectively. So we have what we call the best buyer strategy. The best buyers usually live in the best neighborhoods, so what we teach people is how to reach them, and we have done this with many insurance agents. It's tougher if you're targeting consumers rather than business owners, because you can pick up the phone and dial businesses. The other thing with companies is, of course, that you can get a list by size of the company. There's a website called Zapdata.com owned by Dun & Bradstreet that will allow you to say, "I want companies that are doing $5 million to $10 million in this ZIP code." You can even break them up by type of industry if there's a type of market that you've done very well with.

FELDMAN: *How does a producer, with a list like that, avoid just taking a shotgun approach?*

HOLMES: Number one for any insurance agent is to pick a small group of ideal buyers that you would like to get—maybe it's two hundred, maybe it's three hundred. How much does it cost to market to three hundred people, especially if you're just sending them a letter? Even if it's an elaborate letter, it's a dollar per person, so that's $300 a month. That's not a big marketing budget. If you send to them twice a month, you're talking a $600-a-month marketing budget. If you get one client out of that, it pays for a year's worth of marketing.

You call before and after you send the mailer. And it doesn't matter how many times they say, "No, I'm not interested, I've got my broker, I'm good to go, I don't want any." Fifty percent of all salespeople give up after a single rejection. When you get up to four rejections, 96 percent of all salespeople have gone away, like a puppy being kicked. The top 4 percent of salespeople never give up. They will say, "This guy should be a client of mine, and I am just going to keep marketing to him."

FELDMAN: *So you focus on marketing to business owners. Why do you recommend this strategy?*

HOLMES: In an insurance producer's case, you can do neighborhoods, but you can't make phone calls. But you know, something like 80 percent of the wealth in the US is created by small-business owners, and I'll give you a great statistic: twenty years ago, there were four million companies in America, and they employed two hundred million people. Today, there are twenty-eight million companies. There are way more entrepreneurs than ever before, and those are guys you can call. If I wanted to sell life insurance to people who needed a lot of insurance, I would target the business owner.

Those three hundred high-net-worth individuals are probably underinsured. I'll give you another great statistic: something like 85 percent of all family-owned businesses do not survive a second generation. And the main reason is estate taxes. When the patriarch who started it all dies, the business that is valued at $200 million is not generating the $100 million or $30 million or whatever it is to pay the estate tax.

FELDMAN: *Your second strategy is about crafting a "pre-pitch" to grab people's attention and quickly position you as a solutions provider. Can you explain this further?*

HOLMES: It involves a concept we call the *stadium pitch*. Let's pretend that I put you in front of three hundred wealthy individuals and give you a chance to present to them all at once. Then I would further challenge you by explaining that they would have perhaps fourteen potential strategic objectives. If I asked you what you want to accomplish in that stadium, you'd say, "I want to make a sale." And

I would say, "Okay, what else?" You'd say, "Well, what else is there?" There's plenty more. You need to establish a high level of credibility and expertise so that a potential client would literally say, "That guy is way smarter or more impressive than my current insurance agent."

FELDMAN: *How do you go about putting together a stadium pitch?*

HOLMES: I give them an exercise where I make them write their stadium pitch. They start out writing things like, "Why I'm better at giving you insurance than somebody else," or, "The five ways I can help you better than the next agent can," or, "Why you should buy your insurance from me instead of anybody else," or some other title focused on themselves. So then I make it harder. I say, "Well, all right, let's pretend that I say to your three hundred people that they do not have to stay, and when the speaker gives the title of his lecture, the audience could feel free to get up and leave if they want." I explain this more fully in my book *The Ultimate Sales Machine*, but there is a pyramid of interest in what you have to sell.

So if the speaker says, "Hi, I am going to talk about why I am a great insurance agent and why you should buy your insurance from me," the average person is going to walk out. A slightly more strategic type of approach is, "I'm here to tell you the five ways people are underinsured." Okay, that still sounds as though you are trying to sell insurance. A really strategic title, something that would keep people in the room, would be, "I'm here to tell you the five ways you and your family can be financially devastated." You know what? I'm not leaving if that's the title of your presentation, because I need to hear how my family can be financially devastated.

FELDMAN: *So you're creating powerful emotion to grab their attention, remind them of their need, and prepare them for a solution.*

HOLMES: Yes. So let's say that one of the three hundred CEOs calls for the free report. So I say, "Well, I'm happy to get you that report. I have a lot of information designed to help people be more financially successful; let me ask you a couple of questions so I can make sure I give you the right information." So now I've got permission to ask the guy questions. Remember, the whole focus has to be on them, not on you. If you start by asking what kind of life insurance they have, you just went from being a strategist to someone selling insurance.

FELDMAN: *How does a strategist differ from someone focused primarily on selling?*

HOLMES: A strategist asks, "All right, so you're the first-generation owner of the business—are you planning to pass it on to other family in the next generation, or are you looking to sell the business? Does anybody else in the family work in the business? I know we targeted you by the size of your company, but can you give me an idea of what your business is doing annually and what you pull out of it? Okay, great, let me tell you about this report . . . ." And now I'm going to use that report as my leverage to get the appointment with the guy. I'm going to tell him that we went out and did a million dollars' worth of research. You can say that because it doesn't cost you a million dollars to get a million dollars' worth of research; it just costs you time on the Internet. Then I'd ask, "Do you have children? Well, would it be of interest to create wealth that lives beyond your generation? We work with a lot of people like yourself who have the same goals: they're looking to create generational wealth, to protect their family, to make sure that they are not caught off guard by any kind of financial devastation."

But notice I haven't said "life insurance." I haven't said anything about "in the event of your death" or mentioned any type of product. Because I'm a strategist, and I want to say all the things that are going to make this guy have a meeting. This is how you can quadruple your ability to set meetings.

So then I say we condense these hundreds of pages of research to an executive summary that we can bring to your office. A tactician might say, "I want to come and talk to you about life insurance." A strategist says, "That mailer that we sent you went out to hundreds of business owners just like yourself, and we've had many of them request to see this information, so we are doing a tour and during that tour we can come by your office. This thing takes twenty-eight minutes, and you're going to see a million dollars' worth of research that will make you more financially successful. Do you have your calendar handy? Okay, well, let's look and see when I can get you on the tour." So, Paul, what did I just do?

FELDMAN: *You've got an appointment right there.*

HOLMES: Now let's go to our other strategic objective. Remember I said when you walk out into that stadium, the first thing you want to do is say something that makes people say, "Wow." The way you get the "wow" is by looking at data over time.

You can tell this prospect that twenty years ago the entire population of the United States of America was employed by four million businesses. Then you say, "Take a guess at how many businesses there are today." The prospect is sitting there with no idea, and you click and say, "twenty-eight million." You want to get that guy to say "wow" at least ten times in ten minutes. The way you do that is you find studies on the Internet.

FELDMAN: *What if, in that first phone call, the prospect directly asks what you're trying to sell?*

HOLMES: You say, "Well, we're insurance experts and financial advisors, but at this point this is a public relations effort for us, and we give out this report for free." And you have just gone back to what you want, which is getting information. Then you can talk about the five ways that people can protect themselves. And by the way, three of the five things you teach that person may not have anything to do with life insurance or for that matter any type of insurance.

FELDMAN: *Why is that?*

HOLMES: Because, if you look at it this way—and this one I'm going to steal from Jay Abraham (he's a good friend of mine and a frequent collaborator)—if you look up "customer" in the dictionary, it says, "a person who buys something from someone else." If you look up "client," it says, "a person who's under the care, guidance, and protection of an expert." So you know that's why architects have clients. Lawyers have clients. Accountants have clients. And hopefully you never call your clients "customers." They're clients. They're under your care, guidance, and protection, and if that's true and you're supposed to be an expert, then it should be in the global life of your clients.

FELDMAN: *Your third strategy involves growing your business by hiring salespeople. Finding the right people can be tough, so how do you make this work?*

HOLMES: We call it the "superstar growth strategy." I realized this strategy at age nineteen while working at a furniture store, making $1,000 a week. That doesn't sound like a lot of money now, but it's probably the equivalent of maybe $3,000 a week now. It was like $150,000 a year—because the average furniture store salesman now will probably make at least $100,000 a year, and I wasn't average. I was outselling the next six salespeople together.

"YOU WANT TO GET THAT GUY TO SAY 'WOW' AT LEAST TEN TIMES IN TEN MINUTES."

In this industry, I quickly found myself in a position of authority and I would hire anybody who was a nice guy. I would watch them fail miserably, horribly, and I couldn't get them to get on the telephone. So I started becoming obsessed with what makes a top producer. Then I got involved with Stanford Research Institute, and they had been commissioned to do a study on top sales producers.

FELDMAN: *What did you find?*

HOLMES: Basically, we found there are five key ingredients to a top producer, and since I don't have time to do a full seminar here, I'll do the first two. Number one is empathy—that's the nice-guy thing that I was talking about. They have a natural ability to bond; they're interested instead of trying to be interesting; they're focused on you, not themselves; and they are sincerely interested in your success.

But that trait by itself will absolutely fail in sales without the other side of the equation, which is what we call ego strength and ego drive. And that means that when someone rejects you, you have the self-esteem not to crumble and go away. You believe in yourself and, therefore, that belief in yourself translates to whatever you sell. You become more effective when someone rejects you, and you don't get blown out for the day. You know, when people try to make cold calls and they get any kind of resistance, bam, they're shot for the day—you can't get them back on the phone.

We teach that balance of ego and empathy. If you're looking to hire top producers and you want to get them cheap, get them young and just understand what makes a top producer. It's ego and empathy.

FELDMAN: *As logical as it sounds, not everyone possesses a strong ego and empathy. Can a superstar rely on ego alone?*

HOLMES: You need both. You need self-esteem, so don't think ego is a bad thing, as long as it's balanced. If it's balanced with empathy, that's the perfect blend. We put an ad in that says, "Don't even call us if you don't think you're the best," and then you put the most money you think that person can make, but you put a range. You say, "Earn $50K to $250K," and then it says (here's the key line), "Young or old, if you have the stuff, we'll know." When a guy calls in, say, "The ad said don't even call me unless you think you're the best—why are you calling me?" Then he says, "Well, can you tell me a little bit more about the job?" I say, "Look, that's a long conversation, I'm going to have that conversation only with the candidates I think are worth speaking to, so why should I interview you?"

So then right there I am going to see what they're made out of. You're putting them into an adversarial situation a minute into the conversation. When you start pushing them away, most people will cave and go away. They might start by saying, "I like to sell, and I really like people." And I'd say, "You do sound like a nice guy, but I don't think you'd make it in insurance. It's a tough field." Just say that and leave the silence. And one of two things will happen: One, they will say, "Thanks, bye," and hang up, and then you know what? You don't want to hire that guy anyway. That's how fast he's going to go away when he gets rejected by the client.

But if he says to you, "You haven't even asked me any questions. I'm working at the furniture store right now, and I'm outselling the next five guys at the store." Great. You know that guy can sell. That's the guy you're looking for.

FELDMAN: *The fourth and probably most important step for anyone who owns an insurance practice, or eventually wants to, is being committed to incremental improvements and having what you call "pigheaded discipline" toward an accomplishment.*

HOLMES: We call it "commitment to mastery," and this is a key ingredient. My father was a marine combat instructor, so I started studying karate very, very early. People will ask, "What's the secret to becoming a karate master?" It's not doing four thousand karate moves. There aren't four thousand karate moves; how many ways to kick and punch do you think there can be? It's doing twelve moves, four thousand times each. That's what makes a master. So we picked six areas of greatness, of mastery, and you want to spend an hour a week improving one of those six areas.

Maybe it's appointment setting, closing, or referrals, and every week for an hour you work on getting better at this. And if you're a one-person army, you say, "How can I get better at this?" And if you've got two people, you sit them together and you brainstorm. If you've got three, you sit there one hour a week, no matter what, and you devote time to mastery. Little by little, if you make one incremental improvement a week, fifty-two weeks from now you can literally transform your entire organization.

Final Thoughts

All agents and advisors dream of having their lead generation, marketing, and sales operate like a well-oiled machine, one that delivers consistent and predictable results over and over. And yet too many think they can wing it when it comes to sales. The truth is, no matter how confident and clever you are, you'll never be as successful as you could be without mastering preparation. Knowing your prospects requires you to know their needs, their wants, and their limits. Without that knowledge, your presentation is going to be a sloppy mess.

A top hitter in baseball strikes out 70 percent of the time, yet they get up every time expecting to get on base. How do they stay so confident in the face of so much failure? For one, they practice their technique hundreds of times between games to keep their reflexes sharp. For another, they study each pitcher they're going to face to calibrate their technique and strategy according to their opponent's, thus improving their chances of making contact. In other words, they prepare an answer to the challenges their opponent will likely present.

Due to the fast-paced nature of the sales industry, many insurance professionals don't put in the time to develop and implement systems to do their job more effectively. Systemic concerns are often put on the back burner in order to focus on the daily business at hand. But that kind of misguided utilitarianism comes at a great cost to opportunity. These systems, though painstaking to develop and implement, are the biggest drivers of growth and freedom.

Key Takeaways

Be precise when choosing your sales audience. There's no sense wasting time, money, and energy pitching to people who either can't purchase your product or services or have no need for them. Once you **target** your prospects, use **persistence**. Half of all salespeople give up after their first rejection. After four rejections, 96 percent will give up. Be persistent in learning why a prospect is telling you no and work to find solutions until you can close. "The top 4 percent of salespeople never give up," says Chet.

Create a **stadium pitch**. If you can present to hundreds of people at once, you'll increase your chances of gaining new clients exponentially. Choose a presentation title that focuses on the needs of your audience, rather than focusing on you or what you're selling. Know the top fourteen objections to your product/service and address them in your stadium pitch.

The ability to create a bond with people by empathizing with their situation and needs is paramount to being an effective salesperson. Just as important, however, is your ability to withstand rejection and remain driven to prove your worth to a prospect. A perfect balance of **empathy** and **ego** is what makes a sales superstar.

Commit to mastery. Identify six key areas of greatness related to your sales approach, whether it be appointment setting, closing, referrals, or otherwise, and spend one hour each week working to improve one of those areas.

CHAPTER 8
TRUST ME, YOU'LL SELL MORE

Jeffrey Gitomer

While many of us hate to admit it, we are all salespeople. Whether we are trying to convince coworkers, clients, or our children, we are all selling something. What sets the winners from the losers in sales is knowledge, practice, confidence, and putting yourself in front of the money.

Few will tell you that fact as bluntly as Jeffrey Gitomer. If you don't know who Jeff is, then you should. The man literally wrote *The Sales Bible*, and legions have been flocking to his events to hear his straight talk ever since.

Not many sales trainers in the world can compete with Jeff's personality, and as you will see in this interview, he does not pull punches. While his material and delivery can be quite controversial, there is no one that can say it like he does. To say he is brash and hard hitting might be an understatement, but his advice works in the real world, especially as it modernizes.

He was one of my first interviews for our magazine because he had a tremendous influence on me personally. He knows how building relationships equates to sales, and he knows how to teach the skills to prove it.

But there was an even more important reason to interview him for the magazine. He attributed his success to the words he published. As you'll see in the interview, he says his business grew from the moment he published his first article in a local business journal and he continues to use weekly newsletters, books, published articles, and blogging to reach his audience.

I am also a big believer in the power of words and messaging. My own success is due in large part to crafting marketing messages. The written word, after all, is going to last longer than you are. It goes farther, reaches more people, and draws more people to you than almost anything else can. Not to mention that in today's tech-driven world, writing is an extremely versatile skill to have.

Jeff dismisses some of the traditional sales methods in this interview. Cold-calling, in particular, gets the cold shoulder. He replaces it with some updated tactics such as using Facebook and LinkedIn to network and generate leads. Social media is a theme in a few interviews in this book, as many experts point to it as an intrinsic environment for salespeople and a convenient tool they should be leveraging fully.

But Jeff says social media is just a representation of a salesperson's whole approach. His bigger message is to get involved in the community and build relationships. Go to charity events. Join clubs. Get to know people as people, and the business naturally follows.

When the business comes through the door, though, Jeff warns against asking them for a referral. Engage those people in more personal ways to keep yourself fresh in their minds, and the referrals will happen more naturally.

Salespeople are usually social, but Jeff's interview is a reminder to do that with purpose. So if you are in sales because you love people, then Jeff wants you to do more of what you love.

Jeff also knows about how to make the big cases in insurance sales. It's not because he has sold insurance, but rather it's because he is a perpetual student of selling. So much so that he deconstructed how his own insurance producer sold him. Yes, that old term "trusted advisor" comes up here, but with Jeff, it's not a catchphrase—it's a badge of honor. In this interview, he and I discuss the principles of sales greatness.

A Conversation with Jeffrey Gitomer

FELDMAN: *According to federal data, the average insurance producer is making only $39,000 a year, while members of the Million Dollar Round Table (MDRT) are averaging well over $300,000 a year. What advice do you have for those at the low end who want to hit the MDRT earnings average?*

GITOMER: The first thing they have to do is communicate with all their clients using something other than a birthday card and a phone call to update their information. They have to get out of their old way of selling and communicating. I want my customers to communicate with me or I want the people that sell me stuff to communicate with me once a week, once every two weeks, or at least once a month. That's really number one. Once you begin to communicate with your own contacts and prospects, you are going to find that your phone starts to ring a little bit. Once it starts to ring a little bit, you are going to go, "Hey, this is pretty easy. I want my phone to ring like this all the time." Then you have to take a more proactive stance.

Keep in mind that most of the guys at MDRT broke into that process before the Internet even existed. These are veterans who have been doing it for a long time and may not even be able to open up a laptop, but they have these annuities coming in, they have all these renewals and referrals coming in, and they earn a ton of money as a result of it.

The new kid has to do it a different way. The new kid has to do it online, in social media, and also go out into the community in order to be perceived as a person of value, by speaking and authoring articles.

FELDMAN: *Why do you think so many people fail in the insurance industry?*

GITOMER: Well, there are several reasons. Number one is that they can't take rejection and they have been taught to get rejected. Some idiot stands up and says make a cold call and some other idiot is writing it down and is going to go do it. And even dumber than cold-calling is asking someone for a referral, especially right after you take an application or right after you make a sale. The best way to get a referral is [to] give a referral. If you know your customers, what they like, what business they're in, and you know what's going on in their lives, give them a referral. You see, that requires work and when salespeople, especially insurance salespeople, are not willing to do the hard work that it takes to make selling easy, they fail.

FELDMAN: *For many of our readers, referrals are their number-one source of new leads. When do you think the best time is to ask for referrals?*

GITOMER: There's no best time to ask for a referral, but there's always a best time to ask for another meeting. Have breakfast, have lunch, go to a movie. Go out skating with his family. Just do something to build a relationship and all of a sudden you'll meet other people and never have to actually ask for the referral. I think it's very awkward when an insurance person asks for a referral. Because what you're asking me to do is take my best friends and give them to you. And if the insurance person gets no responses on referrals, that's not a situation, it's a report card. That customer is saying to you that I need to have a better feeling about you before I'm going to refer somebody to you.

FELDMAN: *You've written frequently about your close relationship with your insurance advisor, and you've worked with a lot of different high-end producers in the business. As a consumer, what do you expect from your insurance advisor?*

GITOMER: Well, one of the reasons that I went with my insurance advisor's program is that he had so thoroughly interviewed me and found out about what my real expectations of lifestyle were, where my income was going to come from, and what I needed to maintain that income. However, I want to backtrack and say that before I would answer any of those questions, I had to trust this guy.

FELDMAN: *That's a crucial first step that even accomplished advisors can sometimes rush or assume that they are trusted prematurely because they're so confident in their abilities.*

GITOMER: That relationship took two years to develop before he ever asked me the first question. I considered him my friend because I trusted him. We were sitting across from each other on an airplane and he got me a speaking engagement at the Million Dollar Round Table main platform.

He did that before he ever asked me for a nickel. I didn't meet with him until one year after I did my main platform presentation at the Million

Dollar Round Table. He's one of the top producers and he's a nice guy. And, you know, we have maintained a friendship now for more than ten years.

If you can't gain your client's confidence and trust, why are you bothering? I don't buy insurance policies. I establish relationships with people and we come to some kind of mutual agreement as to what's best for me. If it happens to include an insurance policy, I'm all in. I don't wake up in the morning and say, "Boy, I need some insurance." No one does.

"IF YOU CANNOT GAIN YOUR CLIENT'S CONFIDENCE AND TRUST, WHY ARE YOU EVEN BOTHERING? ARE YOU TRYING TO SELL ME AN INSURANCE POLICY? GIVE ME A BREAK."

FELDMAN: *Do you think the Internet increases the length of time it takes to acquire that trust, or do you think it shortens it?*

GITOMER: Shortens it, and I'll tell you why. Let's say I'm a homeowner and I have an insurance policy with a guy who also sells life insurance. That insurance agent is sending me a weekly email magazine about what the security issues might be in my house, how to keep my attic cool in the summer and warm in the winter, what I need to do to go on the best weekend vacations in my region. Not only am I going to keep that email, but I am also going to thank that guy and forward the email to four or five of my friends.

FELDMAN: *Where does that leave cold-calling? Is that dead?*

GITOMER: I'm not going to say that it's dead, but I'm going to say that it's on life support. If you cold-call a hundred people, you can get two people to be interested in what it is that you've got. And even then, it's a struggle. I don't understand why people are doing this when they could build a LinkedIn or Facebook account.

Or they could join the chamber of commerce and meet people face to face. Or they could give a talk at a civic group like Rotary or Kiwanis where there are fifty people in a room. They could give a talk on "When you die, who gets your money, you or the federal government?" Now, who wouldn't pay attention to that talk?

So I could sit in my room like a jackass and make cold calls all day and complain about the fact that I get rejected ninety-nine out of a hundred times. Or I could give two speeches, one in the morning and one in the afternoon, and reach one hundred people with a valuable message. And I bet I would get fifty leads if I said, "By the way, if you want to learn more about who gets your money, just put the word 'money' on the back of your business card and give it to me and I'll get you some additional information." Some of them would take my call, return my call, and meet me for a bagel in the morning.

FELDMAN: *If cold-calling is dead or on "life support," what about using direct mail for lead generation in today's world?*

GITOMER: Number one, think that the days of sending out a postcard or sending one back from a letter are over? I mean, the post office is going broke. No one sends a letter. Newspapers are going broke because the Internet has taken over, not because the economy is down. Paul, you have a great Internet newsletter. It's a phenomenal piece. It's easy to read. It's very well constructed and you get a ton of visitors every day. That's because there's value in there.

FELDMAN: *I appreciate that. So you're saying you have to raise your profile in your own area, like by speaking, writing articles in the newspapers, and getting free publicity—which you are an excellent person to model after.*

GITOMER: Thanks. I am good at telling my story. I didn't call you for this interview—you called me. As a salesperson, I've learned how to create the law of attraction. That can only be done if you have a public voice. I began by writing. Writing leads to wealth. Every penny that I have made since March 22, 1992, when my first column appeared in the *Charlotte Business Journal*, I can attribute to something that I wrote. And writing also led me to speaking. Because the retired guys that run the speakers' thing at the Kiwanis Club reviewed my column in the paper, they called me and said, "Hey, we read your column, how about coming over to speak?" So I go and meet hundreds of people, some of whom are still my friends today based on giving a speech.

FELDMAN: *It is said that most people fear public speaking more than death. As one of the country's most prolific public speakers, what is your take on that?*

GITOMER: They aren't afraid; they're unprepared. Intense preparation and intense relaxation are the keys. They take away nervousness and breed confidence at the same time. Practice, practice, practice, and make sure that you record and listen to yourself as much as you can stand it. If you don't think it sounds good, it probably won't to your audience either. You also have to learn to relax and remember it's just a speech, not a trial. Intense focus allows you to hone in on the objective rather than the information.

FELDMAN: *Any quick pointers for those who want to learn to speak?*

GITOMER: I would recommend that everyone go out and join Toastmasters. There are plenty of them in your city. It only costs about $27 for six months and you get to give speeches to your peers and get instant feedback on how you did, whether it's good or bad. It's an excellent place to practice, and if you blow it, there aren't any consequences that can kill your career. Anybody can learn how to do it. So become a certified Toastmaster. That's the easiest thing to do.

FELDMAN: *What should insurance advisors be doing to generate their own leads online?*

GITOMER: Well, first of all, they should have their own website and brand it correctly. They need to brand it with their name, not their company name. Or have both and have one point to the other. Number two, they need to mail a weekly email magazine. Number three, they need to have a blog. Number four, they need some presence on social media. They may have a Facebook page; but I don't mean just a Facebook page, I mean a Facebook fan page. I started to build my network on Facebook and after acquiring 4,500 friends that I didn't know, somebody said, "Don't do it that way; get a fan page." I said, "Okay, but now what?" I had no idea.

FELDMAN: *Setting it up is the easy part. You have to continually update it, engage visitors, and promote it.*

GITOMER: Right. You do. I update my Facebook fan page at least twice a day with questions, ideas, and things that help salespeople. If you go to Facebook and type in "Jeffrey Gitomer," you'll see I have two pages. One was my regular one, but I took the picture down; the other one has a picture of me in black and white. If you click on that one, you will see that I have about ten thousand followers. There's tons of content on there. There are questions that I ask. I solicit answers. I give away stuff. I post my weekly column. It's fun.

FELDMAN: *And it takes time, dedication, and hard work to get that done.*

GITOMER: Heck yes, but not as much work as it takes to make a hundred phone calls. And the rejection rate on Facebook is zero.

FELDMAN: *What advice do you have regarding networking?*

GITOMER: Socialize with some potential customer bases by taking your existing customers with you. My insurance agent invited me to the Unity Charlotte Silent Auction and Dinner. A ton of people were there. I'd never been there before and it was really fun. Now I no longer introduce him as my insurance broker but as one of my friends. If you aren't networking four to six hours a week, then you will lose to someone who does. Networking is the ideal way to build relationships. If you don't have a written one-year networking plan, then you need to get one fast!

FELDMAN: *There's a fine line between being a trusted advisor and being a pushy salesperson. Since most advisors don't consider themselves "salespeople," they spend a significant amount of their time obtaining technical* *and product knowledge. The reality is that consumers don't know what they need or want, and it takes persuasion and sales skills to gain trust and motivate prospects to take action. What percentage of time should an advisor spend on sales training versus other types of training?*

GITOMER: Overall, training should be about a third product knowledge, a third sales training, and about a third presentation skills and other personal development skills, such as attitude. So that is a formula right there. Becoming a trusted advisor is not something that you do, it is something that you earn. And if I've earned the status of trusted advisor then I can't get much higher than that. It's up to salespeople to decide that they want to invest in the relationship with the other person and become that trusted advisor. It's not just about insurance advice; it's about life. And I would challenge people who think that they are a trusted advisor to ask themselves if they are being invited into the boardroom or waiting outside in the lobby. Are they invited into their customers' kitchens or sitting out in the living room? It's real simple. How often do people return your calls? There are little guiding lights to tell you you've earned a high level of respect.

FELDMAN: *I have had the pleasure of working with some great insurance salespeople, including my own father, who felt like they didn't need to continue to learn and improve their skills, because they have already achieved success. What is your take on dealing with someone who doesn't think that they need to improve their sales skills?*

GITOMER: The only way that I have been able to crack into the head of a real strong-minded salesperson is by telling them that I don't really care if they know it, I care how good they are at it. So I ask, on a scale of one to ten, how good is your engagement question? If it's a six, I think there's room for improvement. Most salespeople think that if they can get in front of a customer, they can close 90 percent of the time. That is absolutely flawed thinking. If a person really thinks they know it all, they are going to lose to someone who doesn't know everything and is a student. I don't mind people who already know everything. They're the people who are really easy to pass by.

FELDMAN: *What is one thing that I didn't ask you that you think is an absolute must-know?*

GITOMER: If you do not learn how to talk to people with money, you're going to lose. This is a very subtle, unspoken thing in the insurance industry. You're trying to set up a payment of a couple thousand dollars a month or five thousand a month. Think about that for just a second. There are not many people who can afford to make that kind of payment. And maybe the insurance person himself cannot make that kind of payment. So there's going to have to be a lesson in how to communicate with people with money. Not easy to do.

FELDMAN: *How do you do that?*

GITOMER: Hang around civic organizations. Hang around the arts. Hang around places where other people who have money hang. Go to the theater. Go to the opera. Volunteer at local charities. Go to the Heart Association Ball. Join the United Way. There are a thousand things that you can do that will bring you closer to people who have a few bucks, and you really learn how to talk to them over time. Just don't concentrate on their money. I have a ton of friends who have a ton of money and I never talk to them about their money. What we really talk about is their vision. What do they want to do when they finish working? Where do they want to go? How much time are they going to spend there?

"IF YOU DON'T LEARN HOW TO TALK TO PEOPLE WITH MONEY, YOU'RE GOING TO LOSE."

FELDMAN: *Yes. You learn the verbalism and the body language through osmosis. It isn't something you can take classes on. You just learn to spark up a conversation about anything but insurance.*

GITOMER: Anything but insurance. You make an appointment with somebody, then they pay you to talk about it. But if you talk about it at a social event, they will never talk to you again. And if you are giving a talk at a Rotary Club, you can just say to the guy, "Hey, I'm giving a talk tomorrow, want to come see me?"

FELDMAN: *Public speaking is always a great platform for turning strangers into friends and friends into customers.*

GITOMER: That is correct, sir.

FELDMAN: *And you can't shortcut that.*

GITOMER: No, there are no shortcuts to that.

Final Thoughts

One of the biggest challenges for those of us in sales is growing our network and keeping up with it as it evolves. I consider myself lucky to have learned the online game before it became so necessary. It wasn't easy to keep my business afloat in the early years, when the virtual world was more of a barren frontier of chat rooms and homemade webpages than the hardy wonderland of activity that it is today, but I'm grateful that I survived it.

As Jeff pointed out, every salesperson needs to have an online presence—whether a website, a blog, or a well-maintained LinkedIn, Facebook, or Twitter account—but they shouldn't sacrifice their human-to-human networking opportunities in favor of it, either. The digital world may help introduce you to prospects, but you will still need those good old-fashioned people skills to sell them.

At social networking events, there is one thing to keep in mind: be memorable. I don't mean that in the sense that any press is good press, either. Getting fall-down drunk and ending up doing backstrokes in the fountain will certainly get you remembered but obviously not in the way that you want. No one trusts a person to handle their business if they can't even handle themselves. I mean be worthy of being remembered by those in need of your services. Give out trinkets, get involved in local social clubs and your local chamber of commerce, and be able to tell what you do in fifteen seconds or less that's more interesting than "I sell life insurance."

I remember sitting at a hotel bar one night and asking the man next to me what he did for a living. His response has stayed in mind ever since: "I help large companies find ways to save on taxes." He was a corporate insurance salesman, but rather than just repeating his official job title, he had devised a way of telling what his job offered people.

By mastering icebreakers and conversation-enders, you'll navigate social gatherings with much greater ease and with the kind of memorable response that you're looking for lingering with prospects long afterward.

Key Takeaways

Steady Communication

Get creative about the ways you reach out to your customers. The annual birthday card or holiday card isn't going to cut it anymore. Find unique ways to communicate with each of your customers at least once a month, just to keep yourself fresh in their minds. You never know who else may be winning them over if you're not.

Socialize to Capitalize

Whether it's through charity events, social clubs, conferences, meet-up groups, or just acting on chance encounters, the more you interact with people, the better your chances of expanding your business network and landing new business. Plan to network four to six hours a week, take existing customers with you whenever possible, and by all means, have a written one-year networking plan.

Know the Language of Money

Learning how to speak to those with the money to buy what you're selling is essential to mastering sales. Frequent the places and events people with money frequent: civic organizations, theatre, charity balls. Jeff says, "You really learn how to talk to them over time."

CHAPTER 9
SELLING TO THE REPTILIAN BRAIN

Christophe Morin

Did you know that sales stem from the brain stem? They do, according to a growing number of scientific researchers. Over the last decade in particular, advertisers, neuroscientists, and others have teamed up to study consumers' buying decisions. The results have led to a new field of media psychology that offers a revealing look into how our brain processes a sales situation. It's called neuromarketing, and it's now widely used by the world's largest brands to directly reach the part of the brain responsible for decision making.

Neuromarketing is no stranger to controversy, of course. Some refer to it as evil manipulation, while others argue that neuromarketing is a scientific field that explains what motivates people to buy and satisfy the rational, emotional, and survival instincts residing in the "old brain" or "reptilian brain." That's the part of the brain making the real decisions, and it's what Christophe Morin has spent the better part of three decades studying in order to better understand consumer behavior.

Along with Patrick Renvoise, Christophe runs the neuromarketing consulting firm SalesBrain, a first of its kind. They wrote the best-selling guide to consumers, *Neuromarketing*, together, and they've put their research to the test by consulting with companies such as GE, Riverside Company, Cliff Bar, and Code Blue Corporation.

Christophe uses neuroscience to explain that the human brain hasn't evolved much since Roman times. While consumers have more options now than bronze, iron, or stone, most choices are still made in what scientists refer to as our "old brain," which dates back to around 450 million years ago. The "old brain" originated and takes cues from the fight-or-flight mechanisms.

Billions of dollars of research have been applied to this field, but we still have a limited understanding of the human brain as it applies to consumer choices. Understanding the reasons people buy, how they make their purchase decisions, and how sales and marketing professionals can influence consumer desires is the holy grail of the marketing industry.

Christophe is one of the leading specialists on neuroscience in the business world. He is both a researcher and a seasoned business professional. More than twenty-five years of marketing and business development experience instilled in Christophe a passion for better understanding and predicting consumer behavior. He holds a bachelor's degree in marketing from ESC Nantes, an MBA from Bowling Green State University, and a doctorate in media psychology from Fielding Graduate Institute in Santa Barbara, California. He has also served in upper-level executive positions for several successful businesses.

It's safe to say that when it comes to business, marketing, and the latest in neuroscience research, Christophe knows his stuff. In this interview, we discuss how this science works and how it can help significantly improve client communications, presentations, and messaging. Pay close attention as he reveals how the latest findings in neuromarketing can help you get your clients, customers, and prospects to say yes.

A Conversation with Christophe Morin

FELDMAN: *For those not familiar with neuromarketing, would you explain what it is and how it relates to sales?*

MORIN: Most books on sales and marketing tend to tell you the same ideas and tips. So, ten years ago I decided to take a bold risk and look at the possibility of injecting more science into sales and marketing. I noticed that most of the books tell you the same thing: the key to closing a deal is to make sure you're targeting the right decision-maker. But I discovered that selling is not about targeting a person. Selling is about targeting an organ.

FELDMAN: *That would be the brain, specifically the old brain, or the reptilian brain. From what I have read, you say that's where a lot of the buying decisions are made in sales.*

MORIN: That's right. We have not one brain but three. We have a thinking brain, which is the newest part of our brain, called the *cortex*. And we use it a lot to inform decisions, to compute, to create a rationale for a particular decision. But as sophisticated as the cortex is, we don't really rely on the cortex to actually trigger a decision.

Right underneath the cortex, we have what's called the *limbic system*, which is known as the area where we develop a feeling. So this is where we have a gut sensation about a particular decision. We certainly get a lot of information from our stomach, such as the quality of a decision, but that's not where we trigger the decision.

You have to go below the limbic system to an area called the *reptilian complex*, which includes the brain stem and the cerebellum. It's also sometimes referred to as the "old brain." Some people argue it could be as old as five hundred million years. And in that structure—which connects straight to the spinal cord—you find functions that ensure our survival. This is where we control breathing, digestion, and our capacity to stay alert. Attention is controlled in that area. These functions are happening below our level of consciousness. And to our own shock, we discovered that this area, as primitive as it may be, has control over our final decisions. So we are still triggering decisions at the reptilian level, but we are rationalizing them after they've been produced below our level of consciousness.

FELDMAN: *You talk about messages and communicating directly to this part of the brain. What are the best steps to get right into the reptilian brain, the real decision-maker?*

MORIN: Part of step one was to identify the parts of the brain that are most critical in triggering the decision. Step two was, "Okay, now what? Can we indeed develop a language to communicate to that reptilian brain?" It's not about manipulation. This is about finding the way of communicating that is optimized for the brain. And if it's optimized, it will actually contribute to create stronger and better relationships between people. So we developed a language based on science to give you six grammar rules that you can use to create a sentence that the reptilian brain will understand. We call them *stimuli* because we know that these are biologically anchored in the way we respond. They're not just ideas or suggestions. We know that if people use these six rules, or stimuli, they will trigger activity in the reptilian brain that will contribute to the acceleration of a decision process.

7 MESSAGE BOOSTERS
TO SPEAK TO THE REPTILIAN BRAIN

USE "YOU"
Using the word "you" makes your prospects take ownership of your solution.

BE CREDIBLE
Your passion, energy, and conviction can be sensed by the reptilian brain of your audience.

SHOW CONTRAST
Create a sharp difference between the pain your prospects experience before your solution and the relief of that pain with your solution.

TRIGGER EMOTION
Prospects forget how painful their problems really are. Reenact their pain and make it personal.

VARY LEARNING STYLES
Most messages are only auditory. Use the two learning styles, visual and kinesthetic, to keep your audience engaged.

TELL STORIES
Because the reptilian brain cannot differentiate between reality and a story well told, stories are soft but highly effective influencers.

AIM FOR LESS
Make every second, every object, every word of your message count!

The first rule is self-centeredness. It is no surprise that the reptilian brain is truly selfish. Only things that contribute to survival are of importance to this brain. So many times in sales you find that the salesperson is talking about the company and about themselves. In those moments, it takes seconds for the reptilian brain to recognize that this person is not interested in its survival and shuts down. So a very easy tip is to use the word "you." Because whenever you use the word "you," you are actually bringing in that self-centeredness, which is so critical to get immediate attention.

The second stimulus is to use a lot of contrast in the way you present a situation. Why? Because contrast is a signal of importance for the reptilian brain. The reptilian brain is interested in any event that could mark a sharp disruption. That's why we're such suckers for news that seems, intellectually speaking, unimportant. But because it is presented as the most important event by saying, "Breaking news," "Happening now," "Developing story," our reptilian brain gets a sense that it might disrupt our life. So a selling message has to be disruptive—it has to break neutral. We receive ten thousand messages every single day. You cannot have a chance of getting attention if you are neutral. If you say, "Choose us because we're one of the leading providers of . . . ," it won't have any effectiveness on the reptilian brain. It's a neutral sentence.

The third rule is about being tangible, making the message concrete. The brain has a bias for speed and simplicity. At the level of the reptilian brain, energy consumption is a big deal. And energy conservation is essential to enhance survival. So we do not welcome complexity. We do not welcome having to kick-in our new brain to understand a message. We do not welcome a complicated illustration or a lot of text. We're suckers for visuals. We're suckers for touching and feeling an experience and drawing meaning from it. Many of the best salespeople know to minimize what they say and the explanation. They present a prop, an object, or a visual right away in the conversation.

FELDMAN: *Can't you create a tangible sensation through the use of copy? If you're telling a story, can't that reach that part of the brain?*

MORIN: I'm not suggesting that copy never works in sales, but we do not have, at the reptilian level, a desire to read. Reading is a brand new function we acquired about six thousand years ago. At the level of the reptilian brain, we're talking preverbal. So what you find in research around the effectiveness of text is, yes, if people get motivated by a visual or some event prior to the reading, then the words have the capacity to make us imagine, make us cry, make us be afraid, and all of the sensations that are critical for a reptilian brain experience. But selling, for the most part, has to be conveyed preverbally. And we train people, from engineers at GE Healthcare to people who sell insurance, by helping them recognize the need to convince and clarify what it is that they can do for their prospects in seconds, not in minutes. And certainly not by asking people to read a bunch of text.

FELDMAN: *Yes, because that reptilian brain just wants to move real fast through images.*

MORIN: That's right. We have a bias, biologically speaking, for any action that will conserve energy. Some studies have demonstrated that when people read, they burn more calories than if they watch TV. Why do you think we're such couch potato animals when we end up putting ourselves in front of the TV? Because it's a more passive and less energy-consuming activity than reading.

Advertising and marketing spend a lot of money to reach people. Last I looked, it was $450 billion. It's a lot of money but a lot of waste. In a world that is now bombarding us with thousands of messages per day, the brain has a tendency to adjust by putting all of it into a big bucket called white noise. This is why you cannot succeed by whispering.

Now, does that mean you need to be obnoxious? Does that mean you need to scream every single time you want to sell? I don't think so. I think you have to work harder to create relevance and a contrast that will be significant and informative whenever you're selling. In insurance, a lot of that is creating awareness around the possibility that something might happen that could be truly devastating. You could call this fear-selling. But the truth is, most people don't buy insurance unless they connect emotionally with what it does, which is to avoid the worst. And yet, so much selling in insurance has moved into long explanation—a lot of text and smiley faces. You don't typically sell insurance by just showing smiley faces. I'm sorry, but the evidence just doesn't support that. Can you feature pain? Can you sell on fear? Of course you can. And there are ways to do it that do not compromise integrity.

FELDMAN: *So that was three stimuli, what's next?*

MORIN: The fourth one is our pattern of attention, which follows a U-shaped curve. In other words, we are biologically paying attention at the beginning and at the end of any event. And we tend to forget everything in the middle. Now that is something that has been known for a while. That's why we tend to hold our attention for a good trailer or a good ad if the beginning has a good grabber. And we will remember more if there is a good end, or at least an end that helps us capture the essence of an entire event.

Why is our attention dropping in the middle? Well, again, it's because we do not want to remember much. In fact, our brain is much more wired for us to forget than it is for us to remember a great deal. This might strike you as something really strange. But if people have extraordinary memory, usually it's at the cost of being normal in many of their functions. You're familiar with the savant disorder, where some extreme forms of autism come with an extraordinary memory function. If you're memorizing too much, you're essentially pulling those neurons away from decoding facial expressions and engaging in social interaction. And that does not ultimately make for a balanced brain. So we are wired to place attention at the beginning and the end, which is why in selling, you cannot waste those first few seconds. And you have to find a hook that will captivate right away. At the same time, you have to repeat what's important several times. And you have to close, again, in a way that encapsulates the entire information.

You talked about story earlier. And the format of a story typically is based on a strong beginning and a strong end. That's why stories work for our brain. That's why using a story when you sell is so effective. Because it's efficient for the brain. So I talk a lot about the fact that a strong narrative—a strong theme—is a way of helping the brain create a blueprint of a lot of information.

The last two stimuli are really essential to the model and are a big passion of mine. The fact that we're mostly visual—the fifth rule—is essential to the way we react as reptiles. We only understand the reality that the brain can perceive. And the visual sense is the most dominant and the most powerful sense we have. Most of our brain is involved at some level in visual processing. Some numbers I've seen are as high as 50 percent. At any given point in time, 50 percent of our entire brain energy is involved in some sort of visual processing.

This means that when you sell, you have to integrate the fact that visual delivery is more important than auditory. It is more important than what you can write. And yet, particularly in business, so much information is delivered through slides that have lots of text and bullet points, through flow charts that are impossible to understand in just a few seconds, through illustrations that are so abstract that you can't begin to connect and identify the visual to something that you know exists for real. So we have an opportunity to maximize selling so much by just focusing on visual effectiveness. And one aspect of this that I am a big fan of is how you use this power, not just when you are selling insurance but when you're trying to convince people to change their behavior.

FELDMAN: *But what if you sell something that's not a visual, like insurance, since it's not a tangible product?*

MORIN: Right, but their outlook of what happens if they don't buy insurance can be conveyed visually. It's the family missing one member who has passed away. It's the house being flooded. It's all those images that actually convey in just a few seconds what no text will explain to you in minutes. I'm also talking about the physical presence of people. The way they're smiling. The way they're moving. All of this is processed and decoded visually. Studies have shown that the way you move your body is more important than what you say and how you say it. All of that participates in visual delivery, not just images of potential casualties.

The last piece, and the wrapper of it all, is the importance of emotions. We know that emotions are important when you sell. But very few people understand, biologically speaking, what emotions are. Emotions are chemicals that are used by our brain to trigger, literally trigger, more motivation, more movement, and more memory. Now, think about it. The word itself—emotion—gives you a clue. No motion happens without those chemicals. So emotion is not an option. Emotion is the glue of your message. When you sell—whether it's face to face, digital, or print advertising—if you're not able to trigger an emotion, none of this is going to happen. No motion. No motivation. No decision. No memory. It so happens that there are eight basic core emotions. Some are positive. Some are negative.

As humans, we experience more negative emotions than we experience positive emotions. Why? Because it is better for our survival to amplify the negative than it is to look at just the positive. So why does fear-selling work so well? Because we place our attention more rapidly, more urgently, on anything that represents a fear because it can ultimately help us survive. There are a lot of studies on the effectiveness of these different emotions. I tell my client, "Look, I'm not asking you to use only fear. I'm saying that you need to trigger an emotional cocktail of dopamine, serotonin, and endorphins to help your clients trigger a decision." So by the time you look at the six rules, you have the language that is typically used by the best salespeople without even their awareness. But they can be used by others who want to improve their effectiveness.

FELDMAN: *Does having too many choices frustrate the reptilian brain?*

MORIN: The effective sales message builds on a maximum of three claims. In sales, people have a tendency to say, "Hey, here are ten or fifteen reasons why you should buy from us." Well, the problem is the brain does not have the capacity, or the desire, to hold ten pieces of information. So, research shows that you have to limit your talking points, your benefits, to a maximum of three. And you have to sharpen those three so as to create contrast, so as to suggest we're the only company that can offer you ABC. That will be a condition of attention that is central to your effectiveness.

"WHEN YOU SELL—WHETHER IT'S FACE TO FACE, DIGITAL, OR PRINT ADVERTISING—IF YOU'RE NOT ABLE TO TRIGGER AN EMOTION, NONE OF THIS IS GOING TO HAPPEN."

I say three, but that's typically in the context of business-to-business. In business-to-consumer, I say don't even bother to use more than one, maybe two. And make it so powerful, so special, that it will do the pulling for you. It will grab the attention and hopefully give enough juice to the rest of the brain to engage. Make them easy to remember. Using an acronym will help you do so. Having rhyming on your claims can help you do so. There are all kinds of techniques that have been known for decades. They're generally referred to as mnemonic techniques that are on the surface sort of childish. But they work. So don't let your "new" brain censor or judge how simple your message is if it's going to be effective for the reptilian brain. In the context of a fully flushed-out value proposition, I think it's okay to go all the way to three. But in the context of a promo or even a headline, usually you don't have more than one point. That's why headlines suck us into the story. They typically don't have three points in a headline.

FELDMAN: *What makes a good headline?*

MORIN: Few words. Easy words. And wordplays are very effective. We actually have an emotional response to wordplay because we are happy that we've discovered the double entendre of something. It's rewarding our narcissism in many ways. And it creates a little jolt of endorphins. You know, when we laugh, humor is an emotion. And usually it's because of these tiny little moments where our brain is having a little bit of an epiphany.

FELDMAN: *How do you know when you have connected with the reptilian brain and can move on to the next step?*

MORIN: It's typically when people are switching from the emotional phase to the rational phase. It's when people are starting to ask more pointed questions that appear as if they are logical and rational buyers. Typically, it signals that they have actually received the motivation to rationalize. And now what appears to be a logical buy is in fact a buy that has reached the point of rationalization. We are just fundamentally not designed to be rational buyers. We're emotional buyers. But we love to rationalize. And we continue to believe that we indeed have the capacity to be logical buyers. That's sort of the fallacy that you find in all of the research I've done.

FELDMAN: *So people want to believe that they're rational buyers . . .*

MORIN: But they're not. The reptilian brain has already made the decision.

Final Thoughts

If you've ever had a perfect sales pitch suddenly go south, or a situation where your recommendations were a perfect match for the client, but the client still didn't make the buy, then there's a good chance that the reptilian brain had something to do with it. Many people assume that consumers make choices based on sound logic, and that all a good salesperson needs to close a sale is to show the client why the product or service is right for the client. Unfortunately, the latest neuroscience research shows that this isn't always the case. Consumers make choices for all kinds of reasons, many of them irrational.

So it's critical that marketers and salespersons understand what triggers the brain to buy and how marketers can *ethically* influence and communicate with people on a deeper level. The promise of neuroscience as it applies to marketing is that it will allow sales and marketing professionals to deliver more effective and powerful messages and develop unique and memorable presentations that have a major, lasting impact on potential buyers.

Of course, the use of neuroscience in marketing is controversial. While some view the practice as manipulative, others, myself included, see the application of neuroscience to sales as a way of more accurately understanding consumer choices.

Key Takeaways

Keep your marketing **simple**. The brain instinctively wants to conserve energy for survival. Use **visuals** whenever possible because up to 50 percent of the brain is involved in visual processing, so visuals will be understood faster, with less effort. Present no more than three key features or benefits of your product/service. Stick to just one or two if possible, and make sure there is **contrast**—to their existing state of being, to your competition, etc.

Sell with **stories**. Have strong beginnings and strong endings; the brain is wired to forget the middle. Stories make things easier on the brain, as Christophe says, "a strong narrative—a strong theme—is a way of helping the brain create a blueprint of a lot of information."

If you can't trigger an **emotion**, you can't sell. Incite fear, or promise happiness. People buy with their emotions. They only *think* they buy with rationale.

PART III: MARKETING

CHAPTER 10
THE PREEMINENT ADVISOR

Jay Abraham

Preeminence. It's a word born from its Latin root, *praeeminer*, which means, "rise above or excel." Today to be preeminent means to be of high status or distinction—simply put, you're the best in your field. People with preeminence include the president, billionaires, and legendary athletes, such as Michael Jordan, whose preeminence filled stadiums with raving fans and drove fear into the hearts of his opponents.

For insurance advisors, being preeminent is based on empathy. It's about knowing how clients think and feel, building a practice from that understanding, and then fulfilling that need like no one else can.

Figuring out what people want and need is always the hard part. It's easy to imagine devoting many hours and dollars researching the market, surveying prospective buyers, developing a marketing campaign, and so on. But author, executive, and speaker Jay Abraham says you don't need to do that to be the best. In fact, he argues that you can simply tweak the same time, effort, and money you're already spending to get the same effect.

Many business owners go to a consultant because they are successful and want to solve some particular problems to lift their business off a plateau. But Jay urges people to think big and then build a marketing strategy around what they learn when they do.

Jay has learned keys to successful marketing in his decades of direct mail marketing, followed by a distinguished career as a strategy consultant to hundreds of companies. Today, he's a sought-after speaker and best-selling author of *Getting Everything You Can Out of All You've Got: 21 Ways You Can Out-Think, Out-Perform, and Out-Earn the Competition.*

Jay talks about putting the big picture first by remembering your ideology and philosophy and then acting on them. That may sound like a pretty heady idea, but it is an excellent method for rejuvenating yourself *and* your business.

He goes on to encourage us to look at the full horizon of our possibilities. Jay asks very simply, "Why are you accepting your current standard as being the fullest potential possible?"

That is a question we should all have close by. We all have to ask ourselves from time to time if what we are doing in our business is just what we are accepting day to day. It is easy to get caught up in the constant fire extinguishing that we all have in our lives. But if we don't lift our vision above that, then minutia will consume our days.

Thinking bigger was the theme of this discussion, but the best thing about Jay's approach is that it's so accessible. He breaks this down into steps that anyone can follow. While he emphasizes strategy, he also gets into tactics. His example of how testing can make an enormous difference with a slight change is really eye opening.

In this interview, Jay and I explore the important concept of preeminence, which is about distinguishing business, marketing, and advertising as the standard of what is possible.

A Conversation with Jay Abraham

FELDMAN: *Preeminence has always been a key concept of yours. How does that concept apply to business?*

ABRAHAM: The strategy of preeminence is a powerful yet simple strategy that can transform your business or career. It draws people to work with you instead of your competitors. It gives you uncanny insight into what people want and why they act and react the way they do. It turns clients into friends for life. It strengthens your passion and connection with everyone in your life, inside and outside of business.

Preeminence is based on one thing—empathy—but I don't believe one size of preeminence fits all. It's a dynamic concept that has to be translated to the role you are going to play in the market.

You can be a preeminent ice cream vendor because you make a wonderful process out of stopping for ten minutes for a beleaguered adult who is stressed out of his gourd. You acknowledge the person and you make that moment regenerative and nostalgic. You've got to understand what role you are playing.

So I am not at all suggesting that it's the *same* answer for everybody, but there is *an* answer for everybody. There are many examples of mediocre companies catapulting themselves to positions of preeminence by analyzing what it takes relative to their market niche.

FELDMAN: *Can you give us an example of that?*

ABRAHAM: We had a client that was a very large furniture store generating $40 million in business. We saw that they were spending a couple of hundred thousand dollars a month in full-page ads in their newspaper on Sunday. Those ads would drive a finite number of leads into their store.

We wanted to find the easiest first step for the business to make a difference. So that wasn't going to be changing the ad, although we could have done that. It was changing the dynamic that occurred when people walked into the store.

The normal dynamic people are used to is, "Hello, can I help you? Is there something you want?" And most people say no and then there's disengagement and the power is lost, correct?

FELDMAN: *Sure. That is a typical experience in most stores.*

ABRAHAM: We tested thirty-three different ways of greeting people in the store. We used the same lead flow, same person, and the same time so there was no real change other than what they said. We didn't do anything to their business model that might have been intimidating to the business.

The winning greeting tripled the number of buyers from the people who went into the store. So of the two thousand visitors a month, instead of closing 150, they closed 450, three times more. This by doing nothing different other than changing what was said in the beginning of the relationship.

But that's not even the biggest impact. The average sale went up. And *that's* not even the biggest impact. People kept coming back. *That's* not even the biggest impact. People coming back told other people, and it's on and on. And it was only the first thing we changed because we wanted to be nonthreatening to the business.

FELDMAN: *That's an amazing example of big impact occurring from a small change. But I have to ask: What was the winning greeting?*

ABRAHAM: The winning phrase was this: "And what ad brought you into the store today?"

Now, we didn't know this would work, which is why we tested many greetings. I come from a school that understands variability, where we find the different ways to do the same thing to discover the one that will out produce others by as much as twenty-one times. That different method will take the same time and effort with the same interaction and capital and leverage it for as much as twenty-one times better result. But then it gets mind-blowing because that's true of almost every one of the twenty or thirty impact points with customers and clients.

There are so many ways that you can take the same time, effort, and money and multiply and remultiply the yield. The opportunity is fixed—what you do with it is variable.

FELDMAN: *Do you have any idea why that greeting worked better than the others?*

ABRAHAM: We realized that it put control of the selling situation in the hands of the salesperson. The visitor is going to answer, "Well, I'm here for a French bedroom suite." Then the salesperson says, "Oh, is this replacing another one? Do you have French furniture in the rest of your home? Is it a condo? Are you moving in?" And then it's an advisory role.

That ties to being a trusted advisor.

FELDMAN: *That shows the power of testing, because you can stumble on the right answer and figure out the reason later. What else did you do with this client?*

ABRAHAM: It all goes back to *Reality in Advertising*, a book written by the advertising legend Rosser Reeves in which he did all these analyses of ads and commercials. I read this in 1960 and it changed my life. He saw that the community had the same sixty seconds or the same full page for an ad but realized that some of them had five times the impact of another, while others actually had a negative impact. So I learned testing and variability.

So once we had that process working, we moved to their advertisements and began testing new headlines. The headline is really 80 percent of the ad. It can double, triple, quadruple, up to twenty-one times the effectiveness. Then we tested the description of the furniture.

Each one of these tests multiplied the yield. We didn't spend another dime on advertising or on the furniture store. Didn't spend another minute embracing them at the door but we changed the dynamics. In that case, there were about ten different leverageable dynamics.

FELDMAN: *You are well known for the work you have done when it comes to leads and marketing. What is the one thing every one of our readers should know?*

ABRAHAM: I used to be in the lead-generation business—I've done so many things in my life. It was thirty years ago and to this day most people still don't understand. A lead is not a lead. There are different quality leads, different convertibility, leads that turn into different categories or types of business, leads that produce different kinds of referrals, and so on.

Most marketing people and business owners think tactically when it comes to leads, but in order to grow exponentially, you must think strategically. I have found that when it comes to lead generation and marketing you need to have multiple support columns like the Parthenon in Athens. I call this the Parthenon model because it is built around several pillars of activity. It is majestic, strong, stable, sustaining, and robust.

Unfortunately, most businesses have one primary column for lead generation and marketing that leads to 90 to 100 percent of their business. I call this the "diving board," which can only lead to gradual business growth.

If you can move your business from the diving board model to the Parthenon model, you will no longer be dependent on that one primary activity. But it will actually improve as all the others will reach out and impact that one activity.

FOUR STEPS TO GREATNESS

1. KNOW WHAT GREAT LOOKS LIKE, SPECIFICALLY FOR YOU.

2. GET A ROAD MAP TO GREATNESS.

3. DEVELOP YOUR SELF-CONFIDENCE.

4. STAY THE COURSE. SUCCESS IS NOT A STRAIGHT OR EASY ROAD.

"There are four reasons that few if any perform even remotely close to greatness. When you realize how to operate in that rarefied strata of greatness the impact, the performance, the results, the connection, the relevancy that emanate from it is asymmetric. It's geometric."

FELDMAN: *How do you help clients do things differently? Even though they approached you, I would think there is still a reluctance to change.*

ABRAHAM: The first thing is they have to see how much more is possible. They've got to be able to see objectively without being embarrassed or self-conscious about what they are doing now versus what they could be doing differently. And that requires them to sort of travel a little or a lot outside their own world and see what's different.

FELDMAN: *How do you help people see that path?*

ABRAHAM: I say, let's look at your perspective—what's your philosophy on this? That's the first question: What's your ideology? And then the second question is: Why? The third is: How are you acting on it? What are you doing every day? How are you using your time? How are you using your opportunities? What is the driving force? What are alternative ways to do these things?

FELDMAN: *You made the point that the alternative ways of doing things don't have to cost more money, time, or effort. How do you get that point across?*

ABRAHAM: Well, I can use for an example a health/exercise regimen that's very popular now—the P90X.

Everyone basically comes up with a particular exercise regimen. You're going to be a weightlifter or a runner or do yoga or whatever. And this guy did research and found out that's good, but if you break it up and you do different workouts every day, your muscles don't get lazy. You can just multiply the outcome for the same or less effort and it has more sustainability.

But it can't happen until you question, in a constructive way, how you are using the elements of your situation. First, you've got to break down forensically and question what you are doing.

FELDMAN: *What do you mean by breaking it down forensically?*

ABRAHAM: It requires critical thinking, which most people don't do. It requires thinking about every time you have an interaction or just a meeting, discussion, or observation with anyone who has a piece of the puzzle that you don't. It is being able to take a moment of reflection and say, "Wow, what is it about that person and that interaction that was special?"

I'm not talking merely in the context of your profession. If I go to McDonald's and have an extraordinary experience, the first thing that I do is stop in midstream and think, "What did that young woman or man do that was so engaging that I felt special? That they made me feel that they were personally making this meal something wonderful for me or my family? Or they were personally taking care of it?"

FELDMAN: *One of the messages I got from what you have been saying is that it's important to have small successes, learn from them, and move on to the next one. Is that right?*

ABRAHAM: Yes. I had my neck operated on about two years ago. And I used to be just an animal. I had a forty-four-inch chest and a twenty-eight-inch waist and I could do—I'm not saying to be a braggart—but I could do four hundred dips at a time. Now I'm in physical therapy and the therapist asks me to do ten slow push-ups and he makes me feel proud that I can do that. I've got none of the muscle anymore, but I was happy because I had done it. Then he makes me do twelve push-ups and three sit-ups. I used to be able to do eight hundred push-ups. He doesn't say, "Jay, do eight hundred push-ups."

We tell people, "Don't just jump in and do something." Get a context of all that's possible so you can get excited. And that's the stimulus and the carrot that will drive you on. But first, find the easiest, simple change that will require no additional effort.

FELDMAN: *You're talking about vision a little bit there. It seems like some people have a very specific picture, like making $2 million a year and having a ten-person agency in two years. If people are envisioning something like that, is that what you mean or might that be limiting?*

ABRAHAM: There are three implications of what you said. When somebody says something like that to me, I ask, "Why?" And they will say, "Well, because my average person produces $100,000 of profit for me and I want to make $1 million, so I need ten." And I say, "Okay, but what if you could get your average person to produce $300,000 and generate five referrals each month, and you didn't have to have all the overhead?" So the first question is why.

Second is, why are you accepting your current standard as being the fullest potential possible?

Third is when you start shifting their focus to this greatness or preeminence and being value-based. Everyone says, "Well, we give great value." But it's nowhere even remotely close to what it's like to be operating in a preeminent role. Once you infuse your organization with this sense that they are the most trusted advisor for life for not just everybody they sell to but everybody they interact with, it fuses their being with a whole heightened sense of purpose and a whole different distinction.

Then you grow people who have to maximize because they are on a crusade to add value. They know that your organization protects, advises, and contributes so much on a higher level to the prospective client that it's a disservice to that client to allow your competitor to sell to them. It's not because you hate the competitor but because you guys are so much more heightened in what you do for clients. Then you grow faster because everyone is performing at optimum.

It doesn't happen instantly. It's not like the book *The Secret* where you think and you utter some kind of a meditative thing and everything just manifests itself. Nothing happens unless you have a keen understanding of the factors and you do it pragmatically in a way that reinforces your belief in yourself and the process.

But, that stated, why only ten employees when you can have twenty? Most people suspend such a low ceiling of aspiration and performance on themselves because they don't realize how much is possible.

FELDMAN: *How can people realize what is possible and then act on it?*

ABRAHAM: Here's a great quote from Bob Proctor, a coach and speaker. He said, "Most people in business struggle in life with the wrong nonverbalized question." They are tormented with the question: Am I worthy of this? Can I really grow from two salespeople to ten in four years? Can I really grow my income in this commoditized, ultra-competitive market? Can I really compete against these bigger agencies? Can I really stay in the game long enough to retire with security?

He says that when you realize how much more is possible, you will shift the question. It will no longer be: Am I worthy of this goal? It will become: Is the goal worthy of me? Because you can raise your game many times. I've seen people redouble and double again their results once they shifted their focus from mediocrity to preeminence.

It starts with the commitment to yourself that you are not going to accept a fraction of what life has to give you and what you have to contribute to it.

"THIS IS THE CONCEPT OF PREEMINENCE. THAT IS BEING SEEN AS THE MOST TRUSTED ADVISOR IN WHATEVER ROLE YOU ARE IN... PREEMINENCE IS BEING TOTALLY FOCUSED ON ADDING VALUE FOR THE OTHER SIDE AND UNDERSTANDING WHAT VALUE LOOKS LIKE."

FELDMAN: *How does being preeminent transform a business—and a life for that matter?*

ABRAHAM: When you are preeminent, you think of your role as being the benefactor, the multiplier, the creator of value for your client. The reason it's about the client is if you call them a customer, then you've already submitted to the world of marginalization and commoditization.

Look up in *Webster's* the definition of a customer. It's trite. It's someone who buys a commodity or a service. When you refer to them as a customer, it means you are not treating them as anything more than that and you have accepted that you are nothing more than a commodity.

If you call them a client and you see your role as their most trusted advisor for life and you really understand not just abstractly but in a granular way what executing that role looks like, you will start treating them always as a client. When you look up the definition of client, it is someone who was under the care, the protection, the well-being of the market.

Now, am I saying that everybody is going to do it? Of course not. I'm saying the ones who do will inherit the world. They distinguish themselves. They are not price-oriented because they are preeminent. They are seen as the greatest, most trusted source to whom their clients want to turn.

Final Thoughts

I think Jay's message on preeminence is one we could all stand to think more about day in and day out. I know I need a daily dose of that reminder. At the heart of his message is Jay's belief in the power of reputation. If you are known as the most trusted insurance or financial advisor in town, then that certainly translates into more business. But how do you get there? That is the question of how you part company with mediocrity. It starts by reconnecting with what made you and your business special in the first place and then permeating that throughout everything you do and everyone you work with.

Your job as a leader is to be a visionary, not a manager. To remain influential in the relationship your clients and employees have with you, you must be respected by them. You also need a great reputation among them both to hurdle those that may try to undermine you.

It's a truth that played itself out several years ago in my own business, when a lawsuit with former employees threatened to weaken relations with the workforce and erode my client roster. In short, two former employees used stolen information to set up a competitive company and made unrealistic promises to attract our clients. To make matters worse, they began bad-mouthing both the company and me personally to try to persuade our clients to jump ship.

I immediately called a company meeting and told my staff, "They can steal all the information they want, but they can't steal us. They can steal what we know, but having the information doesn't mean they know how to use it."

Not wanting to sink to their level, I never bad-mouthed them back. Instead, I let our results speak for themselves. I won the lawsuit against them, and they're now insignificant in the marketplace. All of the clients we lost came back once they realized we always made good on our promises, while our newly formed competitor couldn't come close. In the end, I increased our communications within the marketplace and was able to help us reach more prospects.

When you look back at your core beliefs and perspective, they don't just ground you, they reestablish a base to make decisions on. And when our actions are aligned with our values, we are more likely to be successful and to feel fulfilled about what we are doing for a living. Preeminence must be maintained, of course, but the only way to ensure that is to consistently remind yourself of what you do that is exceptional and stay true to it. Your reputation precedes you, so why not make it great?

All of the people interviewed in this book have something important to say. What Jay says in this discussion has the potential to change readers' lives dramatically. I will leave you with another quote from the interview that is worthy of a motto:

"Most people suspend such a low ceiling of aspiration and performance on themselves because they don't realize how much is possible."

Key Takeaways

Become a student of **preeminence**. Make a habit of seeking out and studying the people or companies that are doing better than everyone else. Obviously they know something others don't. What is it? When you experience it firsthand, ask, as Jay says, "What is it about that person and that interaction that was special?"

Incorporate the game of **variability** into your sales strategy. Just about everything can be done better, so mix things up regularly to see if you can improve results, even for strategies that are working. Jay suggests the magic number of twenty-one. Experiment with different ways to do the same thing until you find the one that will out produce others by as much as twenty-one times.

Don't use the single-tactic "diving board" approach to marketing. Structure your marketing like the **Parthenon**, with its many columns—or tactics—that make it strong and stable. It's the way to grow exponentially.

Think big and the rest will follow. When you consistently visualize what's ideal instead of what's reasonable right now, you'll eventually grow hungrier and more confident in making your ideal a reality. Don't accept your current standard as your best potential, and don't ask whether you're worthy of a goal when you should be asking if that goal is worthy of you. Remember not to be embarrassed about what you're *not* doing. Just focus on starting to do it.

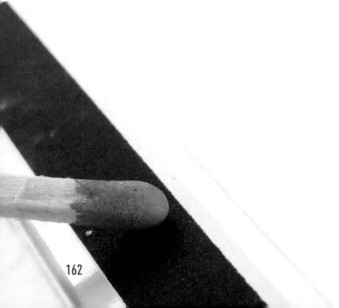

CHAPTER 11
UNCAGE YOUR INNER GUERRILLA

Jay Conrad Levinson

I n today's overadvertised world, it should be harder than ever to reach new clients. But according to best-selling author Jay Conrad Levinson, there has never been a better (or cheaper) time to advertise, market, and promote yourself.

Commonly referred to as the father of guerrilla marketing, Jay has been involved in some of the most recognizable campaigns in advertising history, such as the Marlboro Man, the Pillsbury Doughboy, Allstate's Good Hands, United's Friendly Skies, Morris the Cat, Tony the Tiger, and the Jolly Green Giant. But it's his work as an author and speaker that has made him something of a household name within the business world.

Early in my career, while working at a small company with a commensurately sized marketing budget, I came across Jay's irresistibly titled book, *Guerilla Marketing*. When it debuted in 1983, *Guerilla Marketing* quickly became a revolutionary book that transformed traditional conceptions of marketing and spawned a series of books covering multiple industries and topics. It has since become the best-selling marketing series of all time, with titles from the series selling more than twenty-one million copies worldwide.

Although the name "guerrilla marketing" might convey sneaky and covert maneuvers, the theory is anything but. It's all about using what's at your immediate disposal to capture more business without spending like the federal government.

The basic premise of being a guerilla marketer eschews the wide-net tactics of traditional advertising and focuses instead on reaching smaller, more-targeted populations through a variety of channels. For instance, rather than sending out millions of mailers in the hope of getting a 2 percent response (at best), a guerilla marketer will engage in many different marketing tactics to develop multiple streams of lead generation. Whether it's traditional radio, print, and television channels; social media and Web content; or billboards, benches, and even blimps, guerilla marketers use every technique they can imagine to deliver their message to the right audience.

From Fortune 500 companies to the efforts of a "solopreneur," businesses of all sizes use guerilla marketing tactics to increase the sale of virtually any product, from Bibles to cars to annuities and anything and everything beyond and in between.

In this interview, Levinson shows you how to win whatever battle you are in using guerilla marketing strategies to attract more prospects and generate more leads with little to no out-of-pocket costs. Or, to borrow Jay's words, "achieving conventional goals, such as profits and joy, with unconventional methods, such as investing energy instead of money."

A Conversation with Jay Conrad Levinson

FELDMAN: *For those readers who are not familiar with guerrilla marketing, please explain it and what it can do for them.*

LEVINSON: First of all, I can't think of a field better suited for guerrilla marketing than insurance, so I am excited about this interview. Guerrilla marketing means to go after conventional goals using unconventional means. Guerrillas have to fight war the same way: they want the goal of victory, but they can't use big government budgets to get the tools they need in order to win.

Traditional marketing has always been geared to big businesses, and guerrilla marketing can be geared to small businesses, entrepreneurs, and insurance agents. Even though Fortune 500 companies buy up hundreds of copies of the book at a time to distribute to their sales and marketing people, the soul, the spirit, the essence of guerrilla marketing is small business.

Guerrilla marketing says you've got to focus on your profits. That's the only number that always tells you the truth. Many businesses set new sales records but lose money in the process. Guerrilla marketing is pretty much the opposite of what people think it is. It's not shocking or ambushing and it does not result in instant anything; it's oriented to the client. And it does not work instantly because guerrilla marketers realize, "I've got to build up a sense of confidence, and I can't do that immediately."

FELDMAN: *What makes guerrilla marketing effective?*

LEVINSON: Traditional marketing has always been based on experience in judgment, which is a fancy way of saying "guesswork." But guerrillas cannot afford to make the wrong guesses, so guerrilla marketing is based as much as possible upon psychology, which involves the actual laws of human behavior.

We know that 100 percent of all purchase decisions are made for emotional reasons. People can justify with irrational reasoning, but it was emotions that were behind their decisions. We know the most important thing for an insurance agent, when he or she talks to prospects, is helping them visualize how they will feel after they've made the purchase.

Also, traditional marketing says to always grow your business and diversify. So that leads to companies such as Coca-Cola saying, "Our name means beverages; let's buy a winery," and after they lost nearly $90 million, they thought, "Well, maybe our name means soft drinks." So guerrilla marketing says don't think about diversifying; think about maintaining your focus and adding more excellence. It's hard for people to maintain their focus, but in the life insurance industry it seems that it's mandatory.

Traditional marketing says the way to grow your business is linearly; this means adding new customers one at a time. But that's expensive and slow. Guerrilla marketing says the only way to grow your business in this decade is geometrically; that is, in four directions at once. Enlarge the size of each transaction; have more transactions per year or sales cycle with each of your customers. Also realize that everybody you sell a product or service to is at the center of a network, so tap the enormous referral power that all your clients have. All of these ways cost hardly anything. So you are having larger transactions, more transactions, and referral transactions, and in addition to that, you're growing the old-fashioned way, linearly.

FELDMAN: *What do you say to companies that believe that one strategy or one method is all they need for their marketing?*

LEVINSON: That's nonsense. Advertising and PR don't work the way they used to—and most people never learn that just having a website is a sure path to financial oblivion. So, what does work? Marketing combinations work. If you do advertising and you have PR and you have a website, all three will help each other work.

The days of single-weapon marketing have been relegated to the past; you need to be practicing what guerrillas call 360-degree marketing, which is talking to people from all angles, not just from your website or your ads or your PR. Experiment with which combinations work best for you. People are smarter these days than ever before, especially when it comes to marketing and business. It used to be thought that the intelligence level of the public was on par with that of a twelve-year-old, and now it's thought that the public's intelligence level is on par with that of your mother. Your mother's not going to spend money because of special effects or Flash on a website, let alone because of clever jokes or rhymes. Your mother knows the difference between the sizzle and the steak. She knows to buy substance versus style, though most mothers also occasionally buy style.

FELDMAN: *What about guerrilla target marketing?*

LEVINSON: Traditional marketing aims its messages at groups—the larger the group the better. Guerrilla marketing aims its messages at individuals or, if it must attract a group, the smaller the group the better. There's a new word: *nanocasting*. In broadcasting, let's say you've got a product, Viagra, and let's say you decided to advertise on television because you learned how inexpensive it is now that cable TV is around. You can advertise on television for literally less than $20 on prime time in any city in the United States. This is because of all the cable stations.

So you decide you're going to go on television and you tell the station manager, "I want to advertise my Viagra on your channel." And it doesn't work because you were practicing broadcasting in a way that tries to say everything to everybody, which means you end up saying everything to nobody. So then you get smarter, and you say, "Now I only want to advertise on your stations that are catering to men." See, that's much better, because you're now doing what's called *narrowcasting*. Still, the majority of men don't want Viagra, so you then get smarter still and you say, "I only want to advertise on TV stations where you're addressing men and you talk about health issues." See, now you're smarter. This is called *microcasting*. It still doesn't work well because the majority of the audience is still not your people.

And, finally, you become a guerrilla marketer. You learn the word nanocasting and you say, "I only want to advertise on TV shows that are addressed to men and that talk about health issues; more specifically, programs where they are discussing erectile dysfunction." Nearly

100 percent of that audience is in your market, but because there are so few people, the advertising cost is even less.

Here are some great facts to remember: At any given point, 4 percent of people will buy what you are selling right now. So 4 percent of people want a new insurance policy. All they need to know is which one is right for them and whom they should buy from. Then another 4 percent are ready to buy but they don't know who to buy from, what to look for or what to say, so they need a little more information and then they'll buy.

The other 92 percent are just plain not in the market right now, and guerrillas know to ignore those 92 percent now and to aim at that 8 percent who are the hottest prospects.

FELDMAN: *You have discussed "intentional marketing." What do you mean by that?*

LEVINSON: What's the number-one reason that people patronize McDonald's? Clean restrooms. Good French fries is reason number two. It has nothing to do with burgers or low prices. It has to do with realizing what marketing is all about; namely, any contact you have with your customers—whether it's in the restroom, at your place of business, or with your delivery vehicles—and understanding that you've got to pay attention to all those details. That means everybody who works for you is part of your marketing team because your company will be judged by the employee who treats people the worst. That's why, for example, you have to be sure your phones are answered by somebody who's very good on the phone.

FELDMAN: *The little things make all the difference, and every touch point is important. Do you think businesses need to set standards for intentional marketing?*

LEVINSON: Most businesses don't think about that. I worked for giant advertising agencies pretty much around the world before I did what I'm doing, and we never learned that about the touch points. We never learned about any piece of contact and the importance of the attire worn by your employees or the amount of pierced body parts or tattoos that they see. You're going to be judged by the employees with the tackiest taste.

FELDMAN: *How does a guerilla salesperson go about building a relationship after making a successful initial contact?*

LEVINSON: The best you can hope to do with marketing is to gain people's consent to hear more about your business. That's where the word "opt-in" comes from. Most people will withhold their consent because they have other things to do, but at least 8 percent will give you their consent. Your job is to gain that consent and then broaden it. You start the relationship any way you can, and then you start broadening it, and eventually you broaden it to the point where you can talk to people about why they need this particular insurance policy, right now, at this stage of their lives. But they're ready to hear it because they know you earned their trust.

My wife and I lived in London a couple of decades ago. When we got there, the first purchase we wanted to make was a sound system. We inquired to find out the best place to buy a sound system in London. We also did our homework by looking in trade publications; at the time, there was no Internet. We knew what we wanted. We went to the showroom, looked at the equipment, and I said, "I want this, and this, and this component, and this one and this one." And the manager actually had the gall to say to me, "I'm sorry, sir, I'm not able to sell you those components." I said, "Why not?" He said, "Come here, let's sit down and let's talk." He sat me in a comfortable chair and asked me many questions. When the conversation was over, he said, "You told me what you wanted to buy. Here's what you need: You need this, this, this, and this."

"AT ANY GIVEN POINT, 4 PERCENT OF PEOPLE WILL WANT TO BUY WHAT YOU ARE SELLING RIGHT NOW. SO 4 PERCENT OF PEOPLE WANT A NEW INSURANCE POLICY. ALL THEY NEED TO KNOW IS WHICH ONE IS RIGHT FOR THEM AND WHOM THEY SHOULD BUY FROM."

And it was actually a little bit less money than I was planning on spending. So I told all of my friends, "Go to this showroom because they don't sell you what you want," and that one sale was multiplied many times over from my referrals and so on.

If you sell people what they want and it's the wrong thing, then you're going to get in trouble down the road with bad word of mouth. It spreads faster than wildfire nowadays. With Twitter and Facebook, people talk to lots of people, especially about bad experiences that they've had. Guerrillas do not sell people what they want. They ask questions. They learn about the people and they sell people what they need. And it's hard to say no to what you need.

FELDMAN: *What are some good strategies for insurance producers to develop relationships?*

LEVINSON: If, for example, you've got a potential client who's got a dog and you have a new dog, that's a terrific meeting ground. You can say, "Hey, wait 'til you see my puppy. He's absolutely nuts, and you'll laugh your head off at a couple things he does." Well, another dog owner is going to appreciate that.

It has nothing to do with insurance; it has everything to do with the warm relationship. I remember going to my friend's house and seeing his dog, and it had nothing to do with insurance. I'd like to say I was thinking he was going to bring up insurance, but I knew he wouldn't, because I knew our relationship was beyond that.

FELDMAN: *While it's sad to say, most businesses don't have their own marketing plan, not even a simple one. You've said that a simple marketing plan is better than an extraordinary marketing plan, as long as it gets done. What are some strategies to get a simple plan started?*

LEVINSON: Most people are intimidated by the thought of writing a marketing plan, which is why they don't write it in the first place. That's why a guerrilla marketing plan has only seven sentences. I always say, "Well, all you need to address is seven points."

When I have my students [at Berkeley] create a marketing plan, I give them five minutes to do it. I tell them I've been doing this since 1984, and never before has anyone needed more than five minutes. When I see guys like Steve Jobs or Bill Gates years later, they tell me the marketing plan that they did in my class is still what they're using. Still seven sentences.

If you don't make it simple, people won't do it. The two keys to success in much of life are to have a plan—that's the easy part—and to commit to that plan—that's the hard part. Almost anybody can start with a plan but hardly anybody can commit to a plan. They think marketing brings about instant results.

They get a Facebook account and become active on Twitter. They think the social media will work for them. It doesn't work in a hurry. But if you go about it in the right way, it's not complicated or expensive. The key element is the same one you need in insurance; it is patience, because the best-crafted marketing doesn't work instantly.

Those that are successful had a vision, committed to that vision, and put it into writing because you've got to just start because not having a marketing plan is like entering battle under a commander who says, "Ready. Fire. Aim." It doesn't work if you do it in that order.

You have to be ready, you have to aim, and then you have to fire. And then you have to fire again and again and again. You've got to realize that your competitors aren't going to have as much patience as you are. They're not going to hang in there as long as you. Guerrillas are able to outlast their competitors in the area of patience.

FELDMAN: *How long does it take for a marketing campaign to work and when should you abandon it?*

LEVINSON: Only through experimentation are you going to find out what's working and what's not. And insofar as when to quit, it's not as soon as you think, it pretty much varies, but it's never a short time.

The most successfully marketed brand in history, Marlboro cigarettes, took a year and a half for the company to see that the Marlboro Man was working. Marlboro was doing everything right and, at the end of the year, we felt horrible that everything we had done wasn't working. But they said, "Well, you fellows said that we should hang in there."

So they did, and after eighteen months they started seeing a glimmer that the campaign was working, and their sales have gone up every month since then. It's about patience and it's about realizing that success rarely happens inside of six months.

Eighteen months was a long time. That's longer than it usually takes. But I tell my clients, "Let the person who sees your financial figures be in charge of whether we're going to abandon this. Realize that anything that happens in the first six months is going to be pure luck. After six months, however, you ought to start seeing glimmers that this is working."

The graveyards of marketing are littered with terrific campaigns that were abandoned too soon. People think, "This should work in a hurry," but marketing doesn't. And if you think it does, you're going to be in for a life of grief, frustration, and Tums because it doesn't work instantly; it does, however, work eventually if you commit to it.

Final Thoughts

I am sorry to say that Jay has passed since this interview was published in our magazine. Jay believed that if you could make someone feel good, their business would be regenerative. He had so much passion and energy for lifting others up that he left a trail of encouragement and inspiration wherever he went. I will always remember him as one of the most significant influences on my career and an incomparable innovator in marketing.

He also leaves behind a legacy of incredible work, a trail, if you will, of remarkable ideas that he was always sharing with others. One essential idea that Jay has left us with is that a guerilla marketer's focus should be on profits and exponential growth, rather than the linear growth pattern found in most businesses. There is a discovery process that must take place, of course, but the process of elimination is simple to follow: if one channel or technique works, add to it proportional to the results it yields. You will never achieve massive business growth if you rely on one method of marketing. You need dozens.

Jay believed that guerilla marketers can't rely on one method of marketing. You have to surround your market on all sides using every profitable tool at your disposal. It's okay if leads from one channel cost more than another, as long as it yields enough business to pay for itself.

One marketing practice that I've always liked is the swipe file, which involves tearing out ad copy you love, from anywhere, in order to serve as inspiration for your own marketing. Swipe file marketing allows you to stand on the shoulders of giants. You can compile a library of marketing ideas without the years of effort required to build your own portfolio from scratch. Think of the swipe file as a shortcut.

And if you want a shortcut to the shortcut, try this: buy one of Jay's fifty-eight books and just dive in. You can get started by lifting a few principles and concepts Jay mentioned in this interview. Chief among them, for me, is the idea that when you market your message to no one in particular, you end up saying nothing to everyone.

Consistency in marketing is critical. We're all in the business of marketing our business. The way someone answers the phone, the way you service the client, it's all marketing, which means every employee you have should understand that they're on your marketing team. Every point of contact with a client is a chance to market yourself, and it's a chance to lose a client.

Both prospects and clients need to know what you do for them, so tell them, show them. Be relentless with strategies that work, and don't quit too soon with new ones.

Key Takeaways

Design your marketing so you can **grow geometrically**, not linearly. Adding customers one at a time is slow and expensive. The four directions you need to grow in are: larger sales, more sales, sales from referrals, and yes, continue the traditional method of linear growth as well.

Practice **360-degree marketing**. Reach your prospects from all angles. Experiment with different combinations. They're not going to be moved by a singular flashy technique. Today's buyer is smart.

Make your marketing plan, and stick with it. Your Facebook campaign or other new attempts aren't going to get you results overnight. It takes **patience** and **consistency**.

Utilize **intentional marketing**. Your reputation is only as good as your client's worst experience, so make sure everyone in your company is onboard to present themselves well and provide optimal service. Along with this, make sure you're selling your client what they actually *need*, not necessarily what they're asking for.

CHAPTER 12

THE NO B.S. GUIDE TO ADVISOR SUCCESS

Dan Kennedy

Y ou're still stuck in the 1950s. The whole industry is, according to the man known as the "Professor of Harsh Reality."

But when Dan Kennedy tells you you're wrong, he's right more often than not. And to prove it, he'll just as promptly follow up the accusation with his same rock-solid brand of advice that's given the market edge to companies such as Weight Watchers, Miracle Ear, and Guthy Renker, as well as several insurance companies and top-earning advisors.

This "No B.S." flair has rightfully earned Dan notoriety as one of the world's highest-paid copywriters and marketing consultants, and it is the foundation of his popular books, which include *No B.S. Marketing to the Affluent* and *No B.S. Trust-Based Marketing*.

In addition to his twenty-five book titles, Dan produces what may be the most circulated paid-subscription newsletter devoted to marketing in the world. The truth is, when it comes to marketing, direct response, copywriting, and entrepreneurial success, it's virtually impossible not to come across his name or influence.

As a longtime follower of Dan's, I have been weaving his principles and training tools into InsuranceNewsNet since its inception. In this interview, the professor himself exposes the shocking mistakes agents and advisors make in their marketing and shows you how to get on a path to monumental success. No B.S.

A Conversation with Dan Kennedy

FELDMAN: *You've worked with a lot of advisors over your career. What are some of the challenges you see them face in growing their businesses?*

KENNEDY: I've worked with financial advisors for twenty to twenty-five years, with four or five big product providers and their organizations as well as a lot of independents. The biggest thing that they miss is not unique to them, although the way they mishandle it might be. The mistake is focusing on the product and process rather than on the real ways that a client arrives at decisions about their money. Those decisions are principally driven by who they are going to do it with, not what they are going to do with it.

Healthcare professionals such as dentists make the same mistake. Marketers make the same mistake because we live with our "stuff" day in and day out. We assign a lot more importance to products and process than a prospective client does.

Advisors are constantly defaulting to product, product differentiation, features, benefits, prices, yield, and how this instrument works. The way you can spot an advisor in the woods if you have no other means is that he's going to show you pie charts.

This is not how people reach decisions and, more importantly, have trust and confidence in where they put money. The entire advertising, marketing, selling, and communicating approach is actually at odds with getting the client to the point of purchase and their real goals. You have a sales process in conflict rather than in cooperation.

I had a call two days ago from a private banker seeking an appointment to dazzle me with all of the wonderful things that they can do that my current private banking folks might not be doing. The call was singularly unproductive.

FELDMAN: *Why did that banker fail to dazzle you?*

KENNEDY: For four chief reasons. One, he came at it from a product-centric approach: "I'm with XYZ Company and we do these things and offer these things and put money in these forty-six different things and we do it better and let's get together so I can show you pie charts."

Second, he came from ignorance. One of the things that has changed in all the years that I've worked with advisors is that information about your prospective client has never been as readily, easily, and cheaply accessible as it is now.

When I started in selling, if I had an upcoming meeting with a prospective client and I wanted to research that person, I had to schlep over to the library, get the microfiche files of the local newspapers, and pore through them, hoping to find a reference to this person. If it was B2B business, I'd go to trade journals and look for information about this person. If they had written a book, I'd find it in the library or a bookstore.

Now you can sit in Starbucks with your phone and do a lot of research about somebody. And, although I don't personally use social media, there is a social media presence for me maintained by the companies that are affiliated with me. I also have a website. If you use Google or LinkedIn or Facebook or Amazon or Wikipedia, you are going to find some stuff that you could use conversationally before you ever got on the phone or came to a meeting. But the overwhelming majority of advisors don't.

If advisors are putting on a dog and pony show, waving steak at the door to lure old people into the room at the country club, 99.9 percent of those advisors do not research the people who have registered to be in that room. So there's this enormous amount of unnecessary ignorance built into the selling process as there was in the case of the banker on the phone with me.

Third, there was zero diagnostic questioning. So no probative search for a reason why I should take time and consider doing business with him.

Fourth is follow-up. I'm leaving for England on Sunday for a week of work and so forth. So I deliberately stalled him and inserted myself into his tickler file for a month from now mostly to see what he'll do.

I have great confidence that he will do nothing. I doubt I will get a piece of mail, a book written by him, or a CD with an interview with him on it. If I get anything, I'll get some horrid ad-agency-produced brochure about the bank, which, if you took the name and the logo off, could be a brochure about any other bank.

And this experience with him is the common experience with all private bankers, financial advisors, estate-planning attorneys, and charity annuity salespeople—or to be fair, with about 99 percent of everybody. It's as if nobody has learned anything about advertising, marketing, or selling since the 1950s. There is still a gross overreliance on a shoe-leather, door-knocking, cold-calling, manual-labor-driven process and really poor, unsophisticated use of marketing and advertising.

It dates to a time when media, as well as knowledge about how to use media, were very, very limited. In my work lifetime, FedEx, fax, and the Internet came into being, and I could go on and on and on. And yet, for the most part, all those media were not used by the sales professionals in these fields and are used badly by the companies they are attached to.

FELDMAN: *How do you think insurance company marketing misses the mark?*

KENNEDY: For the most part, it serves three purposes. One, it is more aimed at Wall Street approval than it is at effectiveness in the field. Two, it is satisfying the egos of the C-suite of the companies, so it can appear at the tennis tournament or the golf thing they sponsor. And three, it's mostly plain stupid because it is advertising that ad agencies love because it's unaccountable, not measurable, and all it has to do is satisfy the people paying for it.

But when it gets down to the grass-roots level where John the Advisor has to get this appointment, it has done basically nothing. The companies do their folks in the field no favors and yet waste an enormous amount of money that could be redirected.

The agents themselves have to be much smarter about positioning, advertising, marketing, and selling themselves.

That's not an easy transition. For somebody who has come up as a sales professional, they are deeply ingrained in "kill today, eat today."

To transition from a sales culture to an integrated marketing and sales culture is not an easy thing to do.

FELDMAN: *How can John the Advisor go from a sales mentality to an integrated marketing mind-set?*

KENNEDY: There are a couple of ways. One is to consider the demographic and psychographic makeup of your clients. Who do you have and who do you want?

Then get outside the community of financial advisors and companies and study how nonfinancial businesses market to that same constituency.

For example, if you have fifty-five-to-seventy-year-old, mass affluent to affluent, married homeowners, you can look at companies like Sleep Number beds. They have local brick-and-mortar presence with salespeople but also run very smart and aggressive national direct-response, lead-generation advertising.

So who is doing this well with the constituency that I want to reach?

The second thing is that I would be getting a general understanding of what I frame as direct marketing for indirect marketing businesses.

The third is to forget the accepted norms, which are usually wrong. Most businesses, including this one, are very Amish. Everybody is in a circle looking at each other and mostly trying to farm incrementally better but still farming with a mule and a walk-behind plow. There's enormous resistance to anything that they don't see facing each other inside that circle.

This happens with vendors who specialize in a given industry. I do pro bono work for food banks. There are four or five ad or media agencies that produce most of the direct mail and most of the newsletters for all the food banks in the country.

Consequently, now you have an Amish community with four in it standing in a circle looking at each other. Then they sell their farm implements to the Amish communities standing in a circle around them.

If this were the way that financial advisors operate—absent rogues, renegades, and innovators —every advisor would be going to his appointments with a big pooper scooper to clean up after his horse when he parked outside. And he couldn't meet with anybody after 5 p.m. because there would be no electricity nor could he fire up the laptop to show me that nifty pie chart.

If you want above-average anything, you will not get that by sticking to norms any more than a reformed alcoholic has much of a chance of staying sober if he frequents bars and hangs out with heavy drinkers.

FELDMAN: *I love that Amish analogy. But that being said, I think some people would ask how they can deviate from norms and remain compliant in a highly regulated environment.*

KENNEDY: Advisors have this religious belief that they are the only put-upon, hamstrung, regulated profession or industry in the world. And they feel like they are wearing a crown of thorns and being abused by this and being severely restricted by that like no one else.

And it's entirely untrue. There's virtually no industry—and I work in more than a hundred—without regulatory interference, scrutiny, rules of law, and, in many cases, product provider bureaucracy.

Anybody in e-commerce will tell you their horror shows of Facebook and Google. Anybody in nutrition, nutritional supplements, and most health fields is dealing at least with the Food and Drug Administration, the Federal Trade Commission, the attorneys general in every state, and, in most cases, their own professional associations. Chiropractors and dentists are at odds with the national and state chiropractic associations, and, ironically, even lawyers must combat the compliance dictums of their own bar associations. Pick a business and I'll be happy to show you how it is mired in the same sort of stuff.

Almost without exception—and I've been at this for forty-one years now—people lie about the limits of the actual rules that they must live by versus what they have come to believe are the rules.

The advisor is living inside a pretty small box manufactured entirely of peer standards, industry norms, his beliefs, and, in many cases, his company's compliance officers' beliefs about what can and cannot be done. But that is within a much larger outer box that represents what really can and cannot be done.

I'd rather not mention them by name, but I have a favorite compliance story. Some years ago, I did a bunch of marketing work for a securities company for recruiting but not for public consumption.

Shortly after I delivered all the work, mostly copywriting, the vice president called and said he had bad news. The compliance guys got into it and it's all marked up with all sorts of stuff you can't say and we need you to come into a meeting.

I went to the meeting and we started through all of the stuff they said I can't say within the advisor community to recruit advisors.

And I merrily pointed out to them how much of it I had gotten out of their own corporate brochures and their own material that was actually being used with the public. Often you have compliance people who from one day to the next don't even know what they are doing. They said no yesterday. But they'll say yes today. It depends on their mood.

So the first thing is there's a lot of nonsense about this. When you press and get facts, you find that you have a lot more room to maneuver than most people think they do.

The second thing is neither law nor industry compliance standards preclude doing things differently than everybody else does them. They preclude certain specific ways of doing things.

For example, nothing precludes calling the three-hour evening dog and pony show an Evening with the Authors rather than a seminar or a workshop, as long as the advisor is actually an author. Nothing precludes having a celebrity from the local football team there to greet everybody and sign footballs.

But hardly anybody does it. So the idea that they can't do anything radically different because they are in a compliance-sensitive industry is just ridiculous.

I have a saying that most people would rather have a good excuse than a good opportunity. The reason the vast majority is comparatively poor and at the bottom of their industry in terms of income is not luck. It's attitudinal and behavioral. People prefer their comfortable excuses over uncomfortable and challenging change and invention.

FELDMAN: *Most advisors (and compliance departments) believe and even insist that they can't use client testimonials. You say otherwise. How can we as an industry use testimonials in our marketing?*

KENNEDY: It is absolutely untrue. I have registered investment advisors as clients and we legally use testimonials. There are ways you can't, but there are ways that, very carefully, you can.

The first question is whether you want to figure out a way to do what is effective or if you want to accept the first no you get from a compliance officer, lawyer, product provider, or peer group. Success has a great deal to do generally with how easily you accept being told no.

I can show you example after example of deviation from what the industry views as laws but are, in fact, only norms. For example, I have a financial advisor client who has an annual picture book of clients presenting photographs of and stories about their lifestyle and happiness achievements of the year.

So Bill and Mary, who have always dreamed of buying an RV and touring every state in the union, show pictures and tell stories about that. Clients who have kids graduating from great colleges or similar accomplishments provide pictures and stories about that.

But no one ever explicitly says this is possible "because my advisor Bob makes me so much money or takes such good care of my money." Such words are never uttered. It is merely a celebration of clients' lifestyles and happiness accomplishments. The message, though, is pretty damn clear. You would have to be Stevie Wonder not to see it.

It is a *Chicken Soup for the Soul* book of stories by clients. It is not as good as an overt testimonial, as in, "I went through five advisors who lost all my money and finally John saved me." But it is infinitely better than omitting one of the most powerful categories of marketing tools that there is.

I have another client who in his newsletter regularly recognizes a client's charitable giving and the charity they support. But nothing is ever explicitly said that this is possible "because John the Advisor takes such good care of my money." The message is there, and for his demographic and psychographic, being charitable is a motivation. I started him doing it because the Cleveland Clinic Foundation, which sold me a charitable gift annuity, did a big feature story in their newsletter about me.

Some people trade away their ability to do certain things for the parent company relationship they prefer. As long as they know they're making that trade, I have no problem with it. But there is enormous flexibility in all of this that people too easily ignore.

FELDMAN: *Many of the advisors that I've met over the years say they only work on referrals. What are your thoughts on that?*

KENNEDY: I think they placed an artificial cap on growth. Also, the fact that your best client comes from a referral is somewhat mythical. Sometimes that's true. It's more true that the easiest-to-persuade client may come from a referral, but not necessarily the best one.

In my own practice as a consultant and a copywriter, I would rather not have client referrals. That's because in most cases they haven't gone through my own feeder system and educational process to be really good, appreciative, respectful, trusting, and compliant clients before they get to me.

If an advisor wants to focus on or emphasize referrals, that's fine. But there's a role for integrated marketing and selling. The reason people get less pure referrals than they could is because they don't do referral marketing. They don't really have media and tools and systems and processes for the client to refer into.

Instead, they basically put all the onus on the client: "Here I am. You know I'm doing good work for you. Please tell your friends and family about me." That's asking your clients to be a sales force not a referral source. Very few are really capable of doing that.

Media and marketing play a big role with devices like a good video sales letter that the referring client can tell people to watch. I have a wealth management client who is focused on soon-to-retire or recently retired business owners of companies worth $20 million or more.

In three years, we've gone from him doing a book a year to doing a book every three months, each on a different piece of subject matter related to the clientele. They are largely designed for clients who want to give them to a friend of a family member and say, "Man, you've got to read this book. This is directly relevant to what you and I have been talking about that's going on in your life right now."

So we've lowered the bar dramatically for the referrer. They don't have to have the awkward conversation that they are ill equipped to have: "Man, there's a workshop coming up; how about I drag you to it?"

FELDMAN: *Yes, you can really put your referrals on steroids if you have a whole integrated program and follow-up system. Do you find that the follow-up is often a problem in this business, especially after a seminar?*

KENNEDY: Oh, of course. Here is what I have asked: "Hey, you guys waved steaks at people, got them into a meeting, did your dog and pony show. You had a hundred there and you booked twenty meetings. What do you do with the other eighty?"

Here are the answers I've gotten. Very sheepishly: "We don't do anything." Or, "We dump them into our generic email or mail list and the next time we are feeding everybody steak, they will get an invitation." Or, "Bertha calls them if Bertha has time, but since Bertha doesn't want to call anybody, Bertha rarely has time."

Eighty percent of everything they spent to put people in that room, they throw down the toilet. I've tried to make people uncomfortable with this. I have brought them up in front of the room to tear 80 percent of a $100 bill off and set fire to it because that's exactly what they are doing. There are lots of reasons people don't act immediately. For example, evangelical Christians may have taken a sworn oath to do nothing until they sleep on it.

Follow-up is a way of demonstrating sincerity. I don't buy anything from anybody who doesn't do good follow-up before the sale because that tells me what life is going to be like after the sale.

FELDMAN: *How does an advisor's life change when they adopt the methods that you are describing?*

KENNEDY: It is a much more sophisticated and enjoyable way to do business. Not only will that make life better for the advisor, but it will also actually make this less stressful for the clients.

It will largely preempt the increasing tendency to shop. The Internet is the gift that keeps on giving, but it's also the gift that keeps on taking away by commoditizing the business.

That's especially true with robo-advising, which the Obama administration is pushing. The new fiduciary standard is making it just about impossible for a lot of people of very modest means to get advice from a human. So they can just get advice from a robo-advisor online and they will be just "fine."

Then there is the Google effect. So the advisor's dog and pony show told people about "401(k) rollovers," and then they go home and Google "401(k) rollovers." As they look at all the information that it brings up, basically they age and die before you ever get a chance to make an appointment.

There is a more sophisticated approach: integrating, positioning, advertising, marketing, and selling preempts a lot of this growing nonsense. It's really about becoming the go-to guy. There is a process for this. It is absolutely appropriate for advisors as it is for lawyers, estate-planning attorneys, cosmetic dentists.

It's about developing a trust relationship environment, and advisors would be well served by learning it and elevating the way they play the game.

Final Thoughts

When I first started following Dan's messaging advice, it was the mid-1990s. My company was still young. I was still using Madison-Avenue-inspired ad ideas, but I was unsatisfied with the response. Discovering Dan Kennedy changed my company. I might even say it made my company, because he drove me into the business of marketing and direct response. His seminars, his books, and his prolific newsletters all made me believe that marketing itself was the profitable model for my company. Whereas I had been trying to market my own business, I was now seeing more clearly how I could promote other businesses using my media platform. After all, I didn't make the news; I just sold it.

Nevertheless, common sense is not common practice, unfortunately. My career has certainly been no exception to that fact, and Dan's hasn't either. Like many, Dan is a man made of dualities, a man who lives for the simple things in life, yet thrives in a complex business world. He advocates for the use of social media and technology in marketing, yet he has no Internet at his own home, no personal email or social media presence, and no tech gadgetry of any real significance, either. He prefers cars from the past that have been made to look new again. Just more proof of his straddling two worlds, two eras, all at once.

As Dan understands so well, the tools will change, but human nature will not. Today it's Facebook, tomorrow it will be something else. How you reach people will be different. But the importance, power, and effective practices of *messaging* remain the same.

As soon as I grasped this concept, my own marketing effectiveness soared. What I lost in the glitzy, traditional advertising styles, I gained in creating ads that grab attention and generate huge response.

Dan Kennedy prevailed over very humble financial beginnings, alcoholism, and industry-wide doubts about his techniques and philosophy to become one of the most well-respected and sought-after marketing experts and business consultants of our time. Perhaps knowing this about him makes his lessons even more poignant for me, because I know well personal and business hardships and crushing doubt from within and all around.

Most importantly, I learned how to be more vulnerable in my messaging, to be more direct and sincere, and that by accepting my own personal flaws, I could overcome my business ones as well.

Key Takeaways

Ways to fail in winning a new client include:

1. *Fail by focusing on your product.* Instead, focus on the real ways someone arrives at a decision.
2. *Fail by ignorance.* With the Internet, there are plenty of ways to learn about your prospect before speaking.
3. *Fail by lacking diagnostic questioning.* Ask questions. Find a reason why they need your product or service.
4. *Fail by not following up.* Follow up, and be more interesting than sending a brochure that looks like everyone else's.

Get to know the **demographic** and **psychographic** makeup of your clients. Then see how others are successfully marketing to the same audience.

Diversify your marketing. This means different mediums your message can utilize as well as the different messages you can use that still serve your values and product. Be a rogue, renegade, innovator; don't stick to your industry's norms for marketing. And don't be afraid of regulations and compliance; just find creative ways to work around them.

Avoid referral mistakes. First, a "referral-only" business is not ideal; it caps your growth. Also, referrals often come to you without the relationship-building process you use to win a nonreferred client, which means you haven't groomed them to be an educated "good" client. Don't simply ask for referrals. Use **referral marketing** where your clients pass along a video or some marketing piece that begins to educate the referral properly.

Build a "trust relationship environment." People will always appreciate a human-to-human experience in business, so make a plan for providing a personal touch to your prospects. Whether it's a birthday card, a customized note following a meeting, or just a phone call to follow up, taking a little extra time to let a client know you're thinking of them as an individual can go a long way in gaining or keeping their business.

Brand yourself. Make yourself a class of one by creating media around yourself. It might be a persona, a "celebrity" employee, or just your true self, but finding a way to connect with people is key to influencing people.

Accept your flaws. They are what make you relatable.

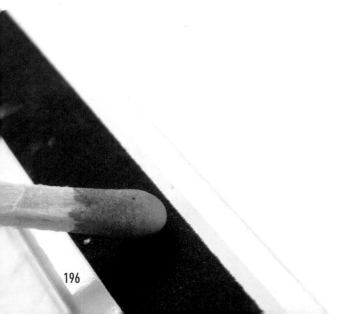

CHAPTER 13
SOCIAL INTELLIGENCE AGENCY

Kevin Knebl

Imagine having the ultimate phone book that provides you with everything you need to know about a company, its employees, and any other prospect you want to do business with. Imagine having access to investigative intelligence surpassing even J. Edgar Hoover's wildest dreams. That is the power of social media, or what Kevin commonly refers to as, "social networking," that can help you close deals and generate new prospects today.

Social media is everywhere, and it's revolutionizing the business world. You can hardly pick up a business magazine or watch the news without hearing about social media. It's become integrated into the lives of your prospects and clients, which means it should be an integral part of your business strategy.

Social media gives marketers and sales professionals access to valuable data about prospects, companies, and even competitors. All of this data is legally and readily available through social media, if you know how to get it.

Most business professionals, however, don't understand social media well enough to effectively profit from the emerging technology. Older professionals who did not grow up using the Internet often don't know how or where to get started when it comes to social media. There is no need to be overwhelmed, though. Social media platforms are really quite simple to use. Unfortunately, driving sales and building brands with social media requires educating yourself and practice.

With so many social media "experts" publishing on the topic, you may think you have already heard everything there is to hear. Think again—Kevin "Obi-Wan" Knebl (pronounced "kanebel") has a novel take on social media. While most experts focus only on the utility of social media in marketing and networking, Kevin has explored the ways in which social media platforms can be leveraged for the purposes of data mining and reconnaissance.

Kevin himself is a mix of dichotomies. He's a native of rural New Jersey, which in itself seems to be a contradiction, and it helped shape him into a fast-talking showman with a core of humble common sense. He was a lounge piano player with a dislike for technology who grew into a sales superstar. Now he's a globetrotting ambassador of the Internet, but he proudly proclaims that he is a hippie in a 44L suit.

In truth, he still harbors a disdain for computers, but he says that's the point. Social media, as he sees it, is not about the media. It's about the social. People who know how to network excel in business, and once you understand the real power in sites like LinkedIn, Facebook, and Twitter, you'll have a powerful set of networking tools at your disposal. People who don't won't have much use for those tools and will lose great opportunities for networking. It's as simple as that. If you're awesome at one-on-one, you'll be in your element in social media. If not, start with the basics and learn to win friends and influence people.

"A professional salesperson today is a mosquito in a nudist colony of opportunity," Kevin has said, and I couldn't agree with him more. But while selling may be harder now than ever, it's also never been easier to gain in-depth knowledge about your client's companies, their preferences, personal lives, hobbies, interests, family members, and friends.

Kevin likes to refer to social media as "the greatest phone book on the planet." What other tool gives you ready access not just to a list of prospects in your area but also to a built-in way to communicate directly with them? Social media can even give you access to the people they know, which can be helpful with getting referrals and introductions.

Whether you are looking for CEOs, doctors, attorneys, veterinarians, or florists in your area, they are all right at your fingertips.

In this interview, Knebl reveals a glimpse at how to mine intelligence and get immediate value from social media.

A Conversation with Kevin Knebl

FELDMAN: *In your book,* The Social Media Sales Revolution, *you say that the landscape is changing for all salespeople. How so?*

KNEBL: Some things, such as technology and its effect on daily activities, will be quite different. But other things will be exactly the same, because it really comes down to human nature.

There have always been good salespeople and not-so-good salespeople. There will always be amateurs and professionals. So, in the future, will there still be people smiling and dialing, trying to get past the gatekeeper and build rapport, asking how-did-you-catch-that-fish-on the-wall, and just saying and spraying and throwing their business cards at people? Yes, because that's just who they are.

But the sales professionals on top of their game will find an even better environment to sell in. That's because people who do very well in sales understand that long-term success is about building and enhancing relationships, not just with your clients and your prospects but also with referral sources who want to do business with you.

God only knows where all these technologies are going, but right now it's easier than ever for people to figure out how to add value using the social media tools available today. But value doesn't always come down to products, services, features, and benefits. It comes down to positioning yourself as a value generator.

FELDMAN: *It's absolutely amazing how much information you can find on potential customers. If you're looking to do business with any company in your area, you could find out who all their employees are, and who their managers are, and you could start from the bottom and work your way up, if you needed to.*

KNEBL: A professional salesperson today is a mosquito in a nudist colony of opportunity. They are surrounded. This is why I say that if you're bad at sales, social media is not a silver bullet. But if you're good at sales, social media is better than a silver bullet. It's the whole gun. It's a cannon.

Because now, as a sales professional, if I'm thinking about selling into a particular company or a vertical, I can learn a great deal about that organization and the people who work there before I ever engage with anybody. The paradox, the irony, is that sales professionals have always done that. Sales professionals have always done their homework. Only now, we have tools that we couldn't even have dreamt of years ago.

Think about it, the more I can learn about someone, the easier it is for me to add value—because I know what his hot buttons are. I know what his triggers are. This is just common sense, but common sense is uncommon. So the more you can learn about your prospects, the easier it becomes for you to become a massive value generator because you're giving them what they want. You're not trying to talk them into something they don't want.

FELDMAN: *Other than what's covered in your book (which is fantastic), what else does one really need to know and understand about social media?*

KNEBL: I think that somebody trying to figure out social media really should be figuring out networking. I'm not a fan of the term "social media," because "media" tends to be a one-way monologue. Billboards are media. Radio is media. TV is media. Networking is a two-way dialogue. It's an interaction. So I prefer the term social "networking," not "social media."

Social networking is combining great interpersonal networking skills with modern communication technology—and modern communication technology is LinkedIn, Facebook, and Twitter. That's all it is. There are a lot of people out there with tape on their glasses and pocket protectors who know all the bells and whistles on social media but they have the interpersonal skills of Hannibal Lecter.

I encourage my audiences to spend some time learning the proper Internet etiquette or *netiquette*. I think it actually goes beyond that, because most people never study networking. I regularly speak to audiences and ask them if they have read *How to Win Friends and Influence People*.

Salespeople are notoriously guilty of winging it, and I can say this because I was a corporate salesperson for years and was the top-producing salesperson in the world for an international consulting company with 320 salespeople in eleven countries. It wasn't because I was a closing ninja. It was because I had some great mentors who taught me it was all about networking and building relationships.

FELDMAN: *Social media tends to be thought of on a mass scale: How many followers do I have, or who am I connected to? You see it as the opposite. You place more value on the individual relationships. How can social media help you with your "offline" relationships?*

KNEBL: I've been teaching social media for nine years, but I've been speaking about networking for seventeen years. Until they started inventing social media, one of the first things I would teach my audiences would be from Harvey Mackay's book, *Swim with the Sharks without Getting Eaten Alive*. That's the Mackay 66, which is a list of sixty-six things you need to learn about your prospects or your clients. It's everything from what college they attended to their favorite booze, to their kids' names and if they like football.

But you're not going to sit down with somebody and go through this list because that would be an interrogation. You would gather this information over time. Mackay taught his salespeople to do that for years and still does. I would tell people to go to Mackay66.com, download his sixty-six questions, and gather data on the people you want to do business with.

So when I first started looking at LinkedIn and Facebook, I said, "Oh my God, all the information that it would have taken us years to figure out I can now find in about three minutes."

I can go to their LinkedIn profile, see where they went to school, see if they like golf, see if they belong to the country club or Kiwanis. I can type their name into Facebook. Now I'm seeing pictures of their wife and kids. I'm seeing pictures of little Johnny, who just got a home run at Little League last week. I'm seeing a picture that Bill just got back from his vacation in Hawaii. As a sales professional, this is the Holy Grail. All this information I now have at my fingertips to build a know-like-trust relationship. In the old days, you had to be a part-time detective to gather as much information as you could.

FELDMAN: *For people working in the business market, what social media channel would you recommend?*

KNEBL: Well, I think there's validity in all the social media platforms, but I would absolutely say to start with LinkedIn. If my territory is a hundred miles from my desk, I could log into LinkedIn and go to the advanced search screen to do a hundred-mile search of anyone on LinkedIn that has CEO, CFO, business owner, or sole proprietor in their job title.

Now I can pull up that entire list and then save it because you can create lists inside LinkedIn folders. Now that becomes a customer or client relationship management tool, and now I can just start looking through it. Not only can I see who these people are, as we already covered, I can see where they went to school, whether they golf, whether they fish.

But more importantly, because LinkedIn works in three degrees of separation and it shows you who you know and who they know, now I can actually see, oh, here are three people in Camp Hill or Harrisburg that I want to get to know, and I happen to know four other people that know these guys. If you get good at networking, people are going to want to introduce you to their friends because they know you're going to add value and not kiss them on the first date.

All roads come back to networking. They always have and they always will. They will even more so now. I could also go onto LinkedIn and type in "Central Pennsylvania business groups" and see all the people that belong to those business groups, and I could just start mining through all that data.

FELDMAN: *Where do most people go wrong with social media?*

KNEBL: They just get on social media and they jump in with, "Buy my product, buy my product, buy my product, buy my product," and then they ask, "How come nobody is buying my product?"

And I say, "Well, it's because you're about as stimulating as a root canal." Just like if you went to a networking meeting and you walked in the room and said, "Hey, here are five of my business cards. Let me tell you what a good lead is for me."

I call that kissing on the first date, and not only is it kissing on the first date, it's using tongue. You don't want to be kissing on the first date. You want to learn how to network effectively.

FELDMAN: *You have a unique way of responding and communicating on an individual basis whenever you connect or are connecting to someone. Can you explain?*

KNEBL: Whenever somebody connects with me on LinkedIn, or accepts an invitation request from me on LinkedIn, or if I accept someone's invitation, I never, ever just pass that person by. I immediately send a reply that basically says, "Hi, Paul. Thanks for connecting with me on LinkedIn. I'm glad we can begin a mutually beneficial relationship. Here are a couple of resources that might be able to help you in some way and add some value to you. I'm all about paying it forward and adding more value to the business community, and I want you to make me prove it. Enough about me. I'd love to learn more about what you do, and if I ever have the opportunity to direct business your way, I'd be happy to help you. How may I help you in some way to your success? Kev."

By the way, the resources that I send, usually just two links to two videos that I've created on YouTube, are in no way designed to sell. It's information that people can use to advance themselves personally or professionally. I could tell you stories for hours, with huge dollar signs, about how that response has led to tremendous revenue.

So if somebody is saying, "Hey, man, nice to meet you. Buy my product. Buy my product. Buy my product," the relationship is over.

Also, just like if you walked up to me at a networking event, face-to-face, with a glass of merlot in your hand, I'm not going to just ignore you when you start talking to me, turn around, and walk away.

But people do it on social media all the time. I call it drive-by friendings, drive-by likes, drive-by follows. Why in the world, if you're sending me an invitation to connect on LinkedIn, would I not extend my hand and say, "Hey, nice to meet you. Here's a little bit about what I do, but I'd like to learn more about what you do."

FELDMAN: *You have a pretty big social media following, how do you respond individually to everyone and keep up?*

KNEBL: I have templates that I keep in LinkedIn, Twitter, and Facebook-related folders on my desktop. The first thing I do when I get up in the morning is I get my cup of coffee, I sit in front of my computer, and I see who sent me an invitation to connect on LinkedIn last night. Then I accept the invitation and I send them my simple template back, with the first name changed to their name. Then that triggers a process of networking that keeps me top-of-mind in front of them without me ever being a stalker, a spammer, or a pest.

It's a gold mine when we actually do it right. People know who you are. They know you, they like you, they trust you, and then opportunities start to show up. But most people would never do that. They'd rather just do a little ego jig. "Oh, somebody else connected with me on LinkedIn. I'm the man." No, you're not. You just have another name in your phonebook, but that doesn't mean you're the man. You're the man when people start interacting with you and go, "Hey, thanks for the reply back."

I don't teach anything that complicated because I'm not that bright. I'm a couple fries short of a Happy Meal. So, it shocks me how few people actually take the time to say to another human being, "Hey, enough about me. I'd like to learn more about you."

"THEY JUST GET ON SOCIAL MEDIA AND THEY JUMP IN WITH, 'BUY MY PRODUCT, BUY MY PRODUCT,' AND THEN THEY ASK, 'HOW COME NOBODY IS BUYING MY PRODUCT?' AND I SAY, "WELL, IT'S BECAUSE YOU'RE ABOUT AS STIMULATING AS A ROOT CANAL."

By the way, here's the million-dollar question I learned from author and speaker Bob Burg: "How would I know if somebody I'm speaking to would be a good prospect or referral for you?" And then I shut up.

Now you'll think I'm the coolest guy on earth because nobody in your entire life has ever asked you that. What they've always said to you is, "Here's what a good lead for me is. Blah-blah-blah. Enough about you. Let's talk more about me."

I have never, in my entire forty-seven years on Earth, had a human being say to me, "How dare you offer to help me! How dare you offer to go out of your way to try to refer me business! Who are you to ask me what a good referral or a good prospect is for me?" No. They say, "Well, let me tell you. A good lead for me is a company that has between ten and five hundred employees, got an annual renewal in October . . . ," and they go on. Now they're telling you everything you need to know to sell them.

FELDMAN: *How much time should people be devoting to keep up with their social media?*

KNEBL: When you get up in the morning, spend fifteen to thirty minutes just building your relationships on social media, then turn your computer off and go do what you should be doing with your sales day. But people don't do that. People treat social media the way they treat a gym membership on Jan. 1—it took me thirty years to get out of shape, and I'm going to get back in shape in thirty minutes. No, you're not. You're going to pull a muscle. You're going to have an aneurysm.

If all you did was spend fifteen to twenty minutes every day for the next 60, 90, to 120 days, you would rekindle or kindle so many relationships. But people won't do it. People are lazy. This is why people who are good at sales will take the time to do the things that make them superstars that the average person will never do.

What do you get when you give phenomenal tools to crappy salespeople? You get crappy salespeople with phenomenal tools. What do you get when you give phenomenal tools to better-than-average salespeople? You get superstars.

Final Thoughts

Building superstar salespeople is a common goal for most business owners and one I've heard about regularly during many of my interviews over the years. Like Kevin, must of us understand that sales is about relationships. People buy from people they like and know. That's what makes social media such an attractive sales tool. Not only can it put you in touch with a prospect, it can also provide deep insight into the person you are meeting with.

But if you've tried using social media as an insurance marketing platform in the past, then you probably already know how challenging it can be. You're not alone. A lot of companies would love to be successful using social media as their main marketing tool. After all, it's free, it's immediate, and it's capable of reaching millions upon millions of people simultaneously. Problem is, very few can find widespread success with it. But why?

One reason is rooted in the fact that people have always wanted to do business with people, not companies. Take, for example, Apple computers. From the time the Mac craze began in the mid-1980s, people weren't just buying computers. They were buying Steve Jobs and his "think different" campaign. They were buying him because he was the face of a philosophy they identified with personally, which happened to also be a company that sold electronics.

In that same vein, social media may be networking on a large scale, but it's still viewed as a very personal territory. That means marketing messages require "small-scale" thinking to be effective.

Marketing on social media is all about having a conversation, not mass-producing an information spew. In other words, users don't want a serious conversation or a generic statement, they want a personal experience. They want to know that you're human, too. So sharing a personal photo or story, a funny cartoon or meme—anything that demonstrates a robot didn't just stamp an ad on their media stream—can do wonders for personal introductions.

Just remember that social media as a platform has the mind-set of a one-on-one connection more than a mass connection. Use it to talk about your story or as a research tool to prepare for a pitch or to design future marketing materials. Whatever you use it for, make sure that when you show up in their newsfeed, you're showing up in an interesting, useful, and relevant way to your audience.

Key Takeaways

Read *How to Win Friends and Influence People* by Dale Carnegie. Kevin reads this timeless classic annually and practices it in his life and with his social media.

Research your prospects. If you want to accurately target your marketing, you need good **relationships**. As with all relationships, the more you know about the other person, the better you can predict and provide for their needs and wants. Just remember not to try to sell to people right away or you'll ruin the relationship before it even begins.

Expand your **social network**. Social media platforms such as Facebook, LinkedIn, and Twitter are great places to get updates on conventions and events, to research your prospects, and to start building relationships. Just remember to ease in slowly so you can remain consistent and get the full impact, rather than burning out after a couple of weeks.

PART IV: PERSONAL GROWTH

CHAPTER 14
ENGAGE HYPERDRIVE

Brendon Burchard

I f you read *Success, Inc., Forbes,* or *Fast Company,* chances are you have seen the ubiquitous full-page ad in which author and motivational speaker Brendon Burchard offers his books free of charge. It's a novel approach to promotion, and it's helped propel his books onto the bestseller lists of Amazon, *Wall Street Journal,* and *The New York Times.* When I conducted this interview with Brendon, his book *The Charge: Activating the 10 Human Drives That Make You Feel Alive* was sitting on the number-two spot on Amazon's bestseller list, just a step behind *Fifty Shades of Grey,* rather strange company for a self-help book but a clear indication of public interest.

Brendon's first bestseller, the novel *Life's Golden Ticket*, came recommended to me by a well-known Internet marketer, a successful businessperson with a larger-than-life persona. When this serious and intrepid businessperson reported that the book literally brought him to tears, I had to go pick the book up immediately, even though I am not normally much of a reader of fiction. Finding the novel excellent and inspirational, I moved on to his nonfiction work.

One can't really understand how good Brendon is at marketing without experiencing it for yourself. I signed up for a free video on his website back in August 2010. In the following thirty-seven months, I received two hundred and thirty-two emails from him, which averages out to about 6.25 emails per month. Such frequency might be annoying if three out of four of those emails were not of educational value, which they are, even though I have time to read only a small fraction of them. Most of them are well-produced videos featuring Brendon.

These videos are like little gems in your inbox. To see and hear Brendon speak is to realize how incredibly energized, engaged, and charged he is as a person. Many of us could have much to learn from him. While reviewing the transcripts and audio from this interview and going through his course, I realized I knew one thing about Brendon for sure: I would love to have a bottle of his energy. I want to always be living the "charged life" of which he speaks.

See, Brendon believes people live one of three lives: caged, comfortable, or charged. Of course, comfort is its own cage. So, caged or free—those are the real choices. A "charged life," according to Brendon, is a life marked by abundance and fulfillment. To live up to our potential in this way, we must understand what drives and motivates us internally. Brendon believes that all motivations can be boiled down to one or more of what he calls the "10 Human Drives." These are subdivided into two categories, the baseline drives (what you need to start your motivation) and the forward drives (what you need to live a charged life). The first step is activating the ten human drives that make you feel alive.

Brendon is clearly an overachiever, a prolific marketer, and an extraordinary teacher. When I spoke with him, his book was topping the charts. His book launch was paired with a larger product launch that included a live event that brought in millions in sales. But according to Brendon, he was driven to write *The Charge* because the "emotional energy of the world has flat-lined" and people aren't realizing their potential of living a "charged life." We are all seeking more from life, but few of us make the changes or take the necessary steps to accomplish more.

If Brendon's philosophy sounds familiar, you might have read his previous number-one bestseller, *The Millionaire Messenger*. You might have also seen him on CNN, *ABC World News Tonight*, Wall Street Journal TV, PBS, and *Oprah and Friends*, or read of him in *Success* magazine, Inc.com, Forbes.com, FastCompany.com, or the *Huffington Post*. He's been on a mission to help people since he survived a serious car crash nearly twenty years ago at age nineteen. Now he claims to be not only one of the world's most sought-after speakers but also the highest paid marketing and motivation trainer. Despite all his success, Brendon still is approachable and grounded in helping individuals find happiness and business success.

Brendon's "10 Human Drives" help remind us that life is not about going fast and blasting past everybody else. Engaging all the important drives he lays out will help you transcend all the stuff that's *supposed* to make you happy and leave your caged life behind.

In this interview, Burchard discusses how to not only live a fully charged life but also how to help others, including clients, do the same.

A Conversation with Brendon Burchard

FELDMAN: *Why did you write* The Charge?

BURCHARD: I wrote the book specifically because I think the emotional energy of the world has flat-lined.

Right now, a lot of people are scared, confused or, even worse, they're in a place where things are going well and they have everything they need to be happy but they're really not. They feel this deep stirring that there is something more. So what can they do with that? How can they transform that?

As soon as they understand their ten human drives and what really motivates them, they live energized and charged lives.

FELDMAN: *In your book, you say people live in that world of fear, and yet we have so much overabundance in this world. Has there been a fundamental change in the human condition and needs over time?*

BURCHARD: Yes, everything has shifted about the human condition. And a lot of biologists and old-school psychologists say you really can't claim that our human needs have changed over time.

I argue that not only did those needs change, they changed dramatically in just the past decade. Where we work has changed from fields to factories to the on-the-go network work force. There are many other recent factors, including how we relate to each other through the Internet, which has also intertwined our work and social lives.

So now we've learned that the old trappings of success—of status, money, power, and wealth—do not move the needle substantially in terms of people's happiness. The world's largest global studies in happiness have proven over and over again that it's not where you live or how much money you make. It's more about your emotional state. It's about your internal charge. The more that you feel fully charged and the more you have clarity and courage within you, the more likely you are to feel happy.

We have to learn how to make that happen not by accident, as in one day we wake up and say, "Oh, I'm happy today," but rather we guide our lives to make them the most fulfilled and engaged.

FELDMAN: *After years of studying neuroscience and psychology, you have identified three types of lives. Can you tell us more about them?*

BURCHARD: We all live three basic types of life and we may live one type or another at different points in our lives. We either live caged, we live comfortable, or we live charged.

When we're living caged, it means we're bound by other people's expectations, our past or our circumstances. We don't feel like we're living our real life. We might be living our parents' life or the life that the past led us into, but we don't feel we have an ability to choose.

You're caged because you stop taking as much action, you stop expecting greatness in life because you become resigned to what others believe about you—the cage they have surrounded you with. You become scared because the times when you have taken a step outside the cage you were judged or you fell on your face. So you decide to limit your movements, limit your progress in life, and accept the status quo.

A comfortable life is obviously much better. You're at a comfortable level knowing who you are; you are making choices in your life and have had success. Comfortable is a good thing, and most people think that's what they want. Except that people who've had comfort for a very long time wake up one day, completely freak out, and have what we call a midlife crisis or worse. They have an internal crisis that says there must be more to life than this.

"THE WORLD'S LARGEST GLOBAL STUDIES IN HAPPINESS HAVE PROVEN OVER AND OVER AGAIN THAT IT'S NOT WHERE YOU LIVE OR HOW MUCH MONEY YOU MAKE. IT'S MORE ABOUT YOUR EMOTIONAL STATE. IT'S ABOUT YOUR INTERNAL CHARGE.

FELDMAN: *Is that when they turn into what you call "chargers"?*

BURCHARD: Exactly—that's where they have an internal crisis that ultimately leads them into becoming chargers. They say I've got everything I'm supposed to need to be happy. I am comfortable, but I'm not happy.

Why? They realize it's because it's not about the stuff. It's not the car; it's not the house; it's not the picket fence; it's not the nice, cushy job. They realize that those extrinsic things aren't the same as the intrinsic rewards of living their passions full out, of doing things that truly engage and energize them.

The funny thing about the psychology of what makes people engaged, happy, and fulfilled is that comfort does not lead to happiness. As a matter of fact, discomfort makes happiness. When we challenge ourselves and engage our brain to the best of our abilities toward an endeavor that we're passionate about, we feel fully charged.

Even in our relationships, we don't want comfort. The deepest, most authentic relationships are actually quite vulnerable, which people find discomforting. But that's the very thing that makes the connection deeper.

FELDMAN: *How can an insurance producer or financial advisor deeply engage with someone in a business situation?*

BURCHARD: The way to get engaged is to decide that this person in front of you is carrying an important message from the world and it's your job to hear it. While we are there for business, this is not business as usual.

You say to yourself that there's a fateful reason that we are here together—I'm going to honor that and I'm going to be fully present right now. My mind is not going to be on my to-do list or on my agenda or what's happening with the kids or how business is doing. My mind right now is fully engaged with this human being in front of me to whom I have to demonstrate that I'm present, that I care, that I understand, and that I am here to serve.

If that comes across to the client or to the businessperson in that situation, then they resonate. Nothing connects us better than emotional presence. When people are in need—and in most business situations, people are in need—and they sense that you are a fully present servant to care for them, to provide products, services, programs that can help them, they see it is a gift to them. And it's unique because most people today are not present. They're so checked out that if you check back in and you're engaged, you'll stand out in front of your competitors like you never imagined.

FELDMAN: *When you're in a selling situation and people are totally disengaged, how do you bring them in? What's a good way of getting connected and engaged with them?*

BURCHARD: Neuroscience has told us that four things most engage people's minds and their bodies and their souls. These four things are the themes that weave throughout *The Charge*.

The first is novelty. One reason they're not engaged is they have heard this pitch before and yours is just another presentation. So you have to think of a different way to present your service or your product that captures people.

That novelty can't be just one thing. For example, somebody trying to sell something might try to do one cute thing and then go back to their usual thing. You have to make the entire approach novel.

The second thing that engages the brain is challenge. When you challenge somebody in appropriate ways, they get engaged because they have to bring their mental resources to addressing it. So, asking questions that get people to think outside their normal response is a great way to engage them.

Another way to engage is creative expression, which is where people share their unique selves. Ask them what creative things they are doing in their lives and what their hobbies are. Asking them to talk about what engages them creatively gets their full attention. One of our human drives is the drive for creative human expression. As soon as you tap that, they start paying attention.

The fourth piece is connection—having a real connection with them. It's really hard to look at someone who is fully present, fully energized, and fully caring and not be in that with them. If that essence, that energy, is in the room for just several minutes, people will gravitate toward it, reply to it, and give it attention.

FELDMAN: *I am not sure that I have ever come across anyone as "charged" as you are. Your energy and passion radiates through your speaking, seminars, and training; it has led to an incredible amount of success for you personally. What is your secret to performing and sustaining a high-performance life?*

BURCHARD: Well, high performance all comes from this—the secret is knowing what it is and doggedly and consciously chasing after it every single day. It's one of those things that people talk about high performance, but if it's a concept, it does no good. But when it becomes something that is tactical, and really, because you can define it and chase it, then it becomes attainable.

High performance is heightened and sustained levels of clarity, energy, courage, productivity, and influence.

I have found that many of the highest performers in the world from the top CEOs to the most famous celebrities to multimillionaires in industries and companies have those things in common. They're incredibly clear about who they are, what they're trying to achieve, and what they're trying to contribute to the world.

They have greater levels of energy than those around them. This gives them more stamina to produce and more ability to influence others. But it isn't some hyper, caffeine-fueled energy. It's a deep energy within their heart and soul because not only are they taking care of their body but they also have the energy that comes from following their passions. Then they're more courageous and they take more bold action than anyone else around them.

FELDMAN: *Fear is definitely something that holds a lot of people back. But you're not just saying people need courage, you're saying they need to have more courage than anyone else.*

BURCHARD: One of the most powerful things in growing your business right now is having more courage than anybody else. Everybody in business is hiding out, holing up, and hoping the economy turns. You've got very little competition that is adding value out there, so if you put your best foot forward and do it with boldness and distinction, you're going to widen the gap. People will never catch up again. But that requires courage.

The next is productivity. People are poorly focused on time management. They are managing so many little tasks each day that they're not really producing anymore. They're not focused on the needle in terms of growing their business or living a better life.

They get stuck in their inbox each day, and their day's over before they know it. Their inbox is nothing but a convenient organizing system for other people's agendas. So they're living their lives based on other people's agendas instead of really being productive.

The final trait is they are very influential. They understand what drives human psychology and how to have a greater level of rapport to develop deeper and more authentic relationships. They not only do incredible things with their marketing and grow their business through their message, but they also lead others. High performers in any genre are always the ones leading the pack.

And all of those things—clarity, energy, courage, productivity and influence—can be activated by understanding human drive.

FELDMAN: *What needs to be understood about human drive?*

BURCHARD: There are two types of human drives: baseline and forward. The baseline drive is the desire for self-knowledge and to connect with our community. This includes the drives for control, competence, congruence, caring, and connection.

This means, for example, that they're competent at what they do, so you help them develop knowledge, skill, and ability so they can be successful. Once you've met the baseline drive, to engage people in terms of their real feelings and their behavior, you have to tap into the forward drives. These are change, challenge, creative expression, contribution, and consciousness.

FELDMAN: *How can small-business owners focus on these drives to help their unenergized employees get charged?*

BURCHARD: Every leader needs to focus on three of the forward drives consistently: challenge, creative expression, and contribution. Challenge is essential to high performance. There has to be something for your team to rally around on a consistent basis to progress toward, to accomplish, to celebrate.

I work with small-business owners all the time, and I ask, "What has your team recently progressed toward, accomplished, and celebrated in the past three months?" They will say that they are always trying to hit their annual goals. But what about quarterly goals? And what are the overarching challenges that we are always marching toward? How do we celebrate that? Nothing will mobilize a team, nothing, greater than challenge.

When Apple decided to take on Microsoft and Dell, those were among the most bold and inspiring times of that company's history. When we are facing our greatest challenges as a country, such as when we decided to go into space to beat out the Russians, we have always had someone we are trying to outpace. And figuring out who that is in your genre and your business is important. But more important is issuing individual and team challenges that demand their greatest ability and focus. That's how you reenergize a team.

They get fully activated when you add the component of creative expression by issuing a challenge for each individual to bring their best unique ideas to the table and give them the autonomy, trust, and decision-making authority to make those things happen.

THE TEN DRIVES THAT MAKE YOU FEEL ALIVE

THE FIVE BASELINE DRIVES

CONTROL
The desire to regulate and influence our overall life experience.

COMPETENCE
The ability to understand, successfully perform in, and master our world.

CONGRUENCE
The conscious creation of a self-image of who you are and who you want to be.

CARING
The ability to be emotionally open to the needs of others and of yourself.

CONNECTION
The desire to relate to and be accepted by others in an emotional and spiritual context.

THE FIVE FORWARD DRIVES

CHANGE
Managing the balance of the desire to evolve and grow with the need for stability.

CHALLENGE
Rising above one's own concept of self, skills, beliefs, and mental and physical capabilities.

CREATIVE EXPRESSION
The intelligent and creative manifestation of one's own true self.

CONTRIBUTION
The wholehearted giving of your unique voice, talents, influence, and perspective in all you do.

CONSCIOUSNESS
Being at peace with and fully present with what is.

Then they need to see that contribution come into real life. There's nothing worse than contributing something and having the idea die in a file cabinet somewhere. Or you contribute something and no one acknowledges it, appreciates it, or celebrates it. That's not a contribution. That's just work.

So those three things—challenge, creative expression, contribution—will light up any team in the world.

FELDMAN: *Those three are critical, but you really need all ten, right?*

BURCHARD: Right. If you've got an entire team and all of their "10 Human Drives" are activated consistently, I'll guarantee your team will outperform the other guy's team who doesn't even know what the ten drives are. It's one of the great distinctions. You can't lead if you don't understand human psychology.

A lot of extraordinary salespeople forget that the baseline drive is everything for their team. That's because extraordinary salespeople usually have their own baseline drives covered—they understand challenge, contribution, and connection. So they're so focused on their forward drive that they forget most people around them are just trying to meet their baseline drive.

They don't give their team enough control or competence or even connection to feel empowered to rock and roll without the leaders. And nothing is worse than higher performers surrounded by an impotent team. Nothing. It will drive them crazy.

FELDMAN: *What do salespeople need to know about human drives and how they influence sales?*

BURCHARD: The sale happens faster in forward drive than in baseline drive. But many of us have been taught to only meet the pains of our customers. And because we're only trying to solve their problem, we forget that what is most compelling to everyone's future is their ambition, not their pain.

So most people are selling on the baseline drives and don't understand why they can't get bigger deals and bigger contracts. It's because they're only speaking half the language of the human experience. If they take customers into the future and help them focus on ambitions, they start to get bigger and better deals. And, fortunately, with that comes even more competent staff.

FELDMAN: *As one of the world's highest-paid speakers, what advice would you give to anyone fearful of public speaking or someone looking for more audience engagement?*

BURCHARD: Most people think that the job of public speaking is to do something. In public speaking you have one job with the audience and that is to raise their ambition. Period. Great leaders know this.

When you have clarity on the ambition and structure your story around that goal of raising this audience's ambition to accomplish something meaningful, then they are inspired and more likely to take the action you suggest. Great public speaking today is really just about authentic sharing, connecting, and raising ambition. That's it.

Your job is to not go up there and be the wild, crazy entertainer. Your job is to talk to people like you talk to them at a barbeque. Now you're just more caring and more compassionate about their journey and you're more compassionate about sharing real value to people.

When getting on stage is a mission of service and not a demonstration of self, then it starts to feel amazing. Like when I step onto the stage, there's nothing in my entire body that's thinking about me. It's about this audience. It's about turning their eyes on. It's about engaging them, moving them, raising their ambition, and helping them become better human beings. And because I'm all about helping them, I don't even focus on myself.

People who hate public speaking are only thinking of themselves. They would not admit it, but that's true. As soon as you stop thinking about self-display and start thinking about social contribution, you can engage them and transform that fear into a true demand to serve this audience. They're nervous because they're thinking of themselves. In all of sales, there's only one real role. That's to raise ambition.

Final Thoughts

From my time talking with Brendon, and especially after attending a few of his live seminars, I got a chance to experience for myself just how powerful he is as a motivator. Like Tony Robbins, Brendon is a natural connector. As I came to learn, he's able to connect with people on such a large scale because he's genuine. He truly seems to want the best for everyone, no strings attached. His social media use alone is an example of that. He has half a million subscribers to his YouTube channel as I write this and another 4.7 million Facebook "likes." Yet his content is not overly self-promotional. He puts out more material than almost anyone I know, all with no commercials on it. His podcast, for instance, is one of the top personal development podcasts on iTunes, and yet there are no commercials.

It's one thing to want to help people, but it doesn't matter that you care if you aren't putting the work in every day to prove it, to actually do something about it. Brendon embodies that idea. He knows that people want genuine help and inspiration, not gimmicks. So he lives the teachings that he sells, always cranking material out into the marketplace, always teaching and encouraging his followers how to pursue their ambitions, and always putting goodness out into the universe to prove it. That's the best-selling tool he can use. By doing what he believes in and serving a purpose greater than himself, Brendon is earning a great living by helping millions of others to better their own lives.

Somewhere inside each one of us, I believe we all know that we must evolve and change to stay energized and grow, but it's still so easy to fall into the trap of feeling like we're different from everyone else. We're not. We are a lot more alike in this world than we are different. Even in different social-economic situations, there are basic similarities between all of us because we're all human.

As Brendon pointed out, the quest for personal and professional happiness requires us to get uncomfortable from time to time. What got you to the present place in your career, whatever it may be, is not enough to get you to the next level. You have to keep pushing yourself to grow and learn. Be charged by a goal, and if you feel depleted, find an external source to recharge yourself. Go to seminars, take classes, challenge your fears, and break the habits of routine. A caged life is a self-fulfilling prophecy. You have to try new things and reflect on those experiences to grow strong enough to break out.

By connecting to a purpose that was bigger than myself, I found the energy to be bolder, stronger, and more creative in my business decisions, which transformed my life in every possible way. People often think too much about the future and regret too much about the past because they aren't living in the present. We all have cages around us, but the worst thing about them is that they're usually self-imposed. If we can get out of those cages, then we can be unleashed and achieve anything we want. At the very least, you should be able to answer the three questions Brendon says we'll all need to answer in the end with confidence: Did I live? Did I love? Did I matter?

Key Takeaways

Rather than caged or comfortable, lead a **charged** life. Find your passion and live it full out.

There are four ways to **engage** people's minds:

1. **Novelty:** Don't just do one novel thing and go back to normal; your whole presentation or campaign must be novel.
2. **Challenge:** Get them outside their normal response.
3. **Creative expression:** Find out what engages them fully creatively.
4. **Connection:** Be fully present and have a real connection.

For **high performance**, you need full **clarity** on who you are what you're trying to achieve, and what you're trying to contribute to the world. You also need **energy** from caring for your body and following your passions, plus **courage**, **productivity**, and **influence**.

Operate in **forward drive** and use the ten drives to get those around you to operate in forward drive on your behalf.

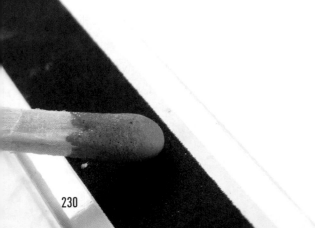

CHAPTER 15
GETTING IT DONE FASTER, BETTER, AND EASIER

David Allen

You know the drill. It's Monday morning and you fire up your computer, only to be greeted by fifty new emails and hundreds of others that you have to get to from the week before. As you start to go through those emails, a client calls you and needs your help. But before you can answer her question, a coworker is at your door, waiting for you to wrap up the call to bring you more demands for your time and attention. Your first appointment is arriving in a few minutes and you haven't had time to prepare adequately. Your day is in a tailspin, and it's not even 10 a.m. By the time noon rolls around, you are already feeling stressed out and you haven't even gotten around to doing anything on your yard-long to-do list yet.

Most of us are given roughly the same amount of time in our lives, and yet some seem to accomplish so much more than others. The reason? Disparities in time management and productivity between workers.

In today's fast-moving electronic age, the pressure to accomplish more (and keep up with what you have to do) is causing unprecedented levels of anxiety and stress in each and every one of us, and the negative effects range from financial loss to mental and physical distress.

So how can you possibly get more "stuff" done in a day without losing all your hair? According to author and consultant David Allen, it's usually a lot easier than people think. Although it does require effort and discipline, the payoff is immense.

I confess that my motivation for interviewing David was a little selfish. He is one of the world's most influential thinkers on personal productivity, and I wanted to see if he could help me "get (more) things done."

According to David, mastering time management "isn't as hard as people think, as long you have effort, discipline, and a system." The same can be said for accomplishing anything in life, but when it comes to time management and personal efficiency, the payoff is exponential—you are accomplishing the task of accomplishing more!

Most of us have the best of intentions. We show up to work intending to do better, but we get so caught up in the day-to-day that we fail to consider the big picture. Planning your day is much more efficient than having the day's workflow dictate the day for you, but the latter is the way most people and most employees approach their work. They let their work tell them what to do.

Business owners and managers must be especially aware of productivity and time management, not just for themselves but for all of their employees. If you can increase your productivity by 10 percent, the results would be great, but if you can boost all of your employees' productivity by the same 10 percent, the difference is exponential.

Unfortunately, it is easy for leaders to overlook time management and productivity at a company, especially since it is not the most-exciting aspect of business. Just bring up time management training in a meeting if you want to see what I mean. You won't be waiting long for everyone's eyes to glaze. But just because something isn't sexy or exhilarating doesn't mean it isn't vital or crucial.

Does the effort put you off? Too busy? Realize this: if you feel like you don't have the time to master time management and productivity, you definitely need this skill more than you think.

In this discussion, David reveals strategies from his best-selling book, *Getting Things Done: The Art of Stress-Free Productivity.*

A Conversation with David Allen

FELDMAN: *When you have so many tasks, people get anxious and don't know what to do first. What's the first thing to gain control?*

ALLEN: The first thing is to do what I call a mind sweep. Without trying to analyze or organize anything, you need to gather in one spot every single thing—little, big, personal, professional—that has your attention. This is anything that's incomplete, anything you've told yourself, "I might, could, should, want to do something about that."

Quite simply, write it down. Go around your office and pull together all the strands and scraps and unread reports and all that stuff. Pile it all in your in-basket.

FELDMAN: *What do you do when you have that list? I've done this and ended up with a mind map that was so big I had to tape six pages together.*

ALLEN: Then you need to go to stage two. You see, you're still at the stage where compulsive list makers have lists stuck all over creation. The next stage is you have to go through each one of those items. What do you say to yourself about each one of those things you wrote down?

FELDMAN: *Well, you would identify them and group them or "chunk" them as well as you could, and mark them off as completed as you did them.*

ALLEN: That response is a typical one. It says, "Wow. The only way I can get relief is to finish everything." Good luck. It's impossible.

You know, the better you get, the better you'd better get. If you went and finished everything, guess what you would have in three days? A bigger mind map of things that you got all excited and ambitious about doing. So there really is a secret here, and it's not about finishing everything. I know it was a trick question because most people don't really realize what they still need to do with their to-do list.

Question number one is, "What is actionable on this list? In other words, what am I committed to doing on this list?" That's the first distinction you need to make.

Stage two is a clarification process. In my book *Getting Things Done*, I call it processing yourself. It is how you empty out your in-basket. In my latest book, *Making It All Work*, I expanded the word to "capture" because it really is about identifying anything that's pulling on your psyche at all, either as a team [member] or as an individual. So now you've captured. Which one of those, right now, are you committed to move on? And believe it or not, there's gonna be a whole lot out there that you say, "No, I can't move on that right now, or I don't want to move on that right now. That's something that will only show up if something else happens before it. Or that's something I'm not sure I have the bandwidth to invest in right now."

A number of nonactionable things show up in your world, and they need to be then identified as one of three things. First, there's trash. Then there is reference material. That's just information I need to keep somewhere so that in case I ever want to loop back around and find it, I have a place for it. And the third nonactionable type is things about which you say, "I don't want to move on that right now, but I might in a couple of weeks." For many of the folks selling out there, that's the old tickler file. So you want to park it in a tickler file and put in some sort of trigger so that it bounces back up.

FELDMAN: *What about the actionable items?*

ALLEN: You need to ask yourself a couple of critical questions. Question number one: What outcome am I committed to? Then that's what I'd call a project. You could call it a prospect in the sales world. But it's something you want to get to some level of closure. Closure means they said yes or they said no. Whatever it is, you want to get finality about that.

Sometimes I'll see things like, "Mom," on to-do lists. And I say, "Well, I know you have one, but why did you write 'Mom' on the list?' If it's her birthday, what are you going to do about it? Give her a party? Then that's a project." Once you say, "Yeah. I'm going to finish this," then the second key question is, "What's the next action?" So outcome and action become the two key questions you need to identify with any email or piece of paper or note you get out of your head. Sooner than later, you need to decide, "Hmm. What exactly am I committed to finish about that, if anything, and if so, what's the next action I need to take to move it forward?"

I guarantee you, anyone reading this right now has a whole lot of stuff on what they would call a to-do list that they have yet to determine what the very next action is. Is that an email to send? Is that something to surf on the Web about? Is that something you need to talk to your assistant about face-to-face? What is that?

FELDMAN: *What are some tricks to getting as many things done as possible, once you've identified the actionable items?*

ALLEN: Let's assume you have your actions. By the way, most mid- to senior-level professionals have between 150 and 220 current "operating next" actions right now. That includes everything you need to talk to your spouse about, everything you need to pick up at the hardware store, all the calls you need to make, all the emails you need to respond to, all the documents you need to draft. The next question is how long would it take to finish any of those? Any of those that you could finish in two minutes should not even be on the list. They should be done immediately. That's the two-minute rule.

Boy, that's a golden rule for productivity. If you're going to ever do anything at all, and it'll take less than two minutes to do it, you're best to do it the first moment you realize it because it'll take you longer to stack it, track it, and review it again than it would to actually finish it the first time it occurs [to you]. And you'd be surprised by how many two-minute next actions there actually are.

As simple as that sounds, most people who start to implement that rule are amazed. If it takes longer than two minutes to do, you don't want to do it right then, because that might be a rabbit trail you shouldn't run down. There may be higher-priority things to be doing. But the next question you need to ask is, if it takes longer than two minutes, should you be doing it? Is there anybody else you can hand this off to? But often, people don't delegate because they haven't figured out what the next step is. If you haven't taken your client notes and figured out what the very next action is with that customer or client or prospect you have, you're the bottleneck. So you need a systemic way to handle that.

The next option is: You're it. The item becomes the part of the inventory of possible things that you need to do. That's still a pretty large list you want to organize. This goes to stage three of getting things under control once you've determined the actions.

If the action is to call Bill Smith, you need to organize a reminder to call him. And we've found over the years that you want to park that in a place where you'll see it when you have a phone and have time, and then you'll make good intuitive judgment calls about what's the best thing to do, given lots of different factors such as how much energy you have. You might not have the energy to deal with Bill Smith right now. You need to do that one when you're fresh in the morning and have lots of horsepower.

FELDMAN: *What are some of the tools to manage all these things that now are in your inventory? Is it technology or just writing things down on a piece of paper?*

ALLEN: All of the above. For the most part, all you need to do to get and stay organized in terms of tools or technology are lists and files. But you need to have the discipline. If you don't on a regular basis review the stuff and keep these lists current, then the system falls away very fast. You might as well not have done it to begin with.

So the fourth stage, which is review and reflect on everything in your system on some consistent basis, is a real key. The weekly review is one of the most critical success factors and behaviors, especially for people out there trying to sell insurance. But you don't sit down once a week and say, "What happened in the last seven days?" and try to catch up.

> ## "IF YOU HAVEN'T TAKEN YOUR CLIENT NOTES OUT AND FIGURED OUT WHAT THE VERY NEXT ACTION IS WITH THAT CUSTOMER OR PROSPECT...YOU'RE THE BOTTLENECK."

Decide what projects have shown up that you haven't had time to think about as a project, and make sure those have been parked in appropriate systems. This is stuff salespeople love to hate, but the really good ones know this is absolutely critical. This is absolutely critical to be able to breathe easy, to have a nice weekend, and to trust that you have all your ducks in a row. Your ducks are going to get out of that row as soon as you walk in on Monday, but you need to have started with a straight row to begin with.

FELDMAN: *What are some strategies for managing interruptions? It's very easy for a producer to be distracted—you're getting calls from clients* *and insurance companies and being interrupted by people in the office and everything else in the world.*

ALLEN: Well, let me give you the hard news first. There are no interruptions; there are only mismanaged inputs. You either shouldn't be getting the input to begin with (why the heck did you pick up the phone?), or it's input that you want to have and you're not necessarily managing it quickly and appropriately. Capturing it, clarifying it, deciding where it goes and how do you park it. If somebody walks into my office and says, "David, da da da da. This is important," and it's potentially meaningful what they're inputting to me, I'm going to take a real quick note right there.

That's why I always have a notepad and pen right in front of me. I take a quick note about that. I say thank you very much. They walk out. I throw that right into my in-basket, and I go back to what I was doing. Why? Because that in-basket will be zeroed out within the next twelve to twenty-four to forty-eight hours max. And I've caught a placeholder of what that potentially meaningful input was, appropriately.

So all I did was switch my focus rapidly. I wasn't interrupted. I got new input. I just managed it appropriately. If I didn't do that—if they walk in and go, "Blah blah blah" and I don't trust my ability to keep track of it or my ability to have a systemic way to manage that potentially meaningful input, guess what I am going to do? I'm going to have to deal with that right then and get annoyed at them for disturbing my world.

There are no interruptions. There are opportunities to influence your world in ways you didn't expect. Frame it that way.

FELDMAN: *Great way of looking at it.*

ALLEN: For most organizations, the big pressing issue at the C-suite level is meetings and emails. But the problem isn't meetings and emails, guys. What are you going to do? Shoot the messenger? Just get rid of emails and meetings and see what happens to your competitive edge.

So why are they complaining? They're complaining about meetings because they are unfocused. They're a waste of time. People don't manage what happens in them. It's the wrong people in the meeting. Nobody's focused on the outcome they were trying to produce.

Often, meetings are there because people don't trust their own systemic way to manage communications and agreements with themselves, so they figure they've got to get a meeting. And the whole thing just self-perpetuates.

FELDMAN: *What other issues do you see most with salespeople?*

ALLEN: Quite frankly, the issues are the same for everybody. What I don't do is tell good salespeople how to be good salespeople. They probably know that. What they need is more bandwidth to be able to do it. So a lot of what our [system] does is free them up. Well, what do you think salespeople feel like they need to be freed up from?

FELDMAN: *Paperwork.*

ALLEN: Yeah, paperwork. A lot of these people are saying, "God. I've got to sit here and fill out this form? You know, I've got business to do. Don't they want me to go sell?"

As good salespeople know, it's really all about relationships, and so obviously anything that helps build trust in the relationship is important. And that's why it's important to implement your own self-management system so you're not letting things fall through the cracks. You're following through on things. You're helping the clients. The clients are always as out of control as your salespeople are anyway.

And if the salesperson can be a little bit more in control than the client, you have a good upper hand and you can lead them.

I have a very good friend—and he happens to be my insurance agent— who has used my system. He used it all the way up to going through the horizons of focus, which I talk about. It means thinking things like, "Wait a minute, what business are we really in?"

And as opposed to selling insurance, he's now an educator. He just reframed his job: "My job is just to educate people. Let them make the choices." Turns out he's selling a lot more insurance because people have to have it, but they want to feel informed. They want to feel like they're making good decisions and that they haven't been manipulated.

And all that still rolls down to "Okay, now what are the projects I have?" Now I need to have a project about informing my clients about this new spin that happened out there, like, "Here's data. Here are your choices. Here are your options."

That will take a different spin based upon whether people are company people, like the New York Life agent selling only New York Life, or an agent or broker who can offer people lots of choices. But they're still really in the same kind of business. It's all about relationships. It's all about education. A good consultant is selling, getting people to focus. But, again, a lot of your good salespeople know all that. They know the selling process. It's just that they usually need to be liberated to be able to do their best work.

Final Thoughts

The more successful we get, the more complicated our lives become. When it does, it's easy to start future-pacing or living in the past. Don't do either. If yours begins to feel like an endless list of to-dos and to-don'ts, take time to focus on what's most important right now.

Believe me, I know that's harder than it sounds. Organization has always been my biggest personal challenge, which only compounded as my company grew and my responsibilities in the office and at home increased.

That's why I found the concept of **mind mapping** to be such a useful tool in managing my time more efficiently and getting more done in the process. There are a million things to do as a business owner, and if we keep them in our mind rather than write them down, it takes up mental energy. Once I put everything I need to do down on paper, I'm always immediately relieved to see exactly what I need to do or want to do and how I can resolve many of the tasks more easily than I may have feared.

The first step to organizing your mental "junk drawer" is simple. Just take an inventory of everything you're responsible for and want to get done.

Once you have written your list, identify the tasks that are both the least time-consuming and the most important to you. Complete those items first by either doing them yourself or finding ways to outsource them; if it's a task you either can't get done or would rather not waste time doing yourself, ask someone else for help or weigh the options to pay someone else for help. The more you can check off your list, the more clarity and mental energy you will free up to focus on more time-consuming or difficult tasks.

Ideas are a dime a dozen and worthless if you don't act on them, but you have to know what all of your ideas and choices are before you can feel confident that you're acting on them in the right way. Capture them, clarify them, and then figure out what to do with them.

Many of us, maybe even most of us, do not feel efficient enough in the office. In my case, despite my constant struggle for self-improvement and my best efforts to systematize my life and delegate more, I still wish I could accomplish more. The work life can begin to feel like a treadmill despite our best efforts to be more efficient. The better we get at managing our time, as David says, "the better you'd better get."

Time is one of the few things that money can't buy. Donald Trump, Bill Gates, and Warren Buffet all have the same amount of time in a day as we do, and yet they often seem to accomplish so much more than we do. It is up to each of us to make the most of our finite time in this world. Better time management means making a conscious and directed effort to maximize every hour of every day that we have been blessed with.

It's possible to have an overwhelming number of things to do and still function productively with a clear head and a positive sense of relaxed control, if you have the right system in place. As with developing any system or skill, that means both actively doing and actively learning. And in this case, your job, company, responsibilities, and maximum potential depend upon it.

Experts like David will tell you that good time management starts with defining a task and then asking yourself how much time, energy, and resources you need to do it and whether it is immediately "actionable." From there, you process the task for completion by setting a priority—do it now, do it later, delegate it, delete it, or file for much later. Where a task lies on that spectrum is dependent upon how important the task is, how much time you have, and how long the task will take. As you get used to doing things this way, the process will become second nature.

Key Takeaways

Sweep your mind. Write down all of your thoughts and ideas so you're able to organize them along with the scraps of papers on your desk, the emails in your inbox, etc., which make up your "list."

Identify **actionable** and **nonactionable** items. Break actionable items down to things you can do now, things where something else must happen first before you can take action, and things you simply don't have the bandwidth for right now. Nonactionable items could be trash, information for reference, or items you want to take action on later and need to put in a tickler file.

The two-minute rule is the golden rule of productivity. If it can be done in two minutes or less, do it immediately, because you'll spend more time than that listing and filing it.

Prioritize your daily, weekly, and even yearly tasks. Decide what needs to be done and how much time each item will take to be most efficient at managing your time. If you can delegate a task, do it. For everything else, label it as something you need to do **now, later,** or **much later**. Always **keep your lists current** and review them once a week.

CHAPTER 16

HOW TO BE THE MOST FASCINATING PERSON IN THE ROOM

Sally Hogshead

S ally Hogshead knows how to fascinate. If you have ever seen her present
on stage, you know how engaging she is.

She is a leading expert on capitalizing on your innate traits and
skills. In fact, she can even tell you how she made a positive out of having what
would seem to be the unfortunate name of Hogshead.

Sally bases her philosophy, presentations, and books, such as *How to Fascinate*, on a personality test she developed. But unlike other tests, Sally's does not determine your aptitude or how you perceive others. Instead, it helps you learn how others perceive you.

The results show seven personality traits, or what she calls "advantages" or "triggers." The top two triggers form your personality "archetype." For example, if your lead trigger is Power and your secondary trigger is Prestige, then your archetype is the Maestro. That means, "Confidence is one of your greatest assets and you waste no time in accomplishing your goals," according to Sally. "Never wanting to settle, you are ambitious and always looking for ways to improve. People admire your unwavering conviction."

Once you align with your archetype, you amplify your power to fascinate, Sally says. To fascinate is not merely to be interesting, by Sally's definition, but to become the center of intense focus. She advocates this insight not just for individuals but for groups as well, arguing that once we know each other's archetype, we can interact more effectively and be more successful as a whole.

The test gave me some surprising insight that got me thinking more about how I lead. I suggested that others in my company take the test, which everybody did with enthusiasm. Soon people were trading their archetypes like business cards. It got us all thinking more about how we interact with one another. Perhaps even more importantly, we had a new appreciation for the strengths within our group.

So I can attest to the test's effectiveness. But if you are still not convinced of this test and analysis, I'll let Sally tell you herself:

"When you fascinate somebody, not only do they listen to you but they want to become involved. They want to learn more, stay loyal, refer you, and talk about you. They want to be more than just a customer. They want to be an advocate."

If you take Sally's Fascination Advantage test, you'll identify which of the seven fascination triggers you use most, with the top two triggers shaping your personality. In Sally's book, *Fascinate: Your 7 Triggers to Persuasion and Captivation*, she explains the triggers and the forty-nine personality archetypes formed by the combination of the test-taker's top two triggers. Once you know this archetype, she says, you can operate at your best.

She is working on a new book, *How the World Sees Us*, which further helps people understand not only their own archetype but also how to deal with the archetypes in other people. But you don't need to know every prospect's archetype to understand what motivates sales. What is important for the purposes of sales, however, is to understand how you can make yourself fascinating to others.

In this interview, Sally discusses how the triggers draw in prospects and keep them as happy clients for years to come.

A Conversation with Sally Hogshead

FELDMAN: *Why is fascination important?*

HOGSHEAD: Fascination is an intense, emotional focus. When you're fascinated by people, you are completely focused on what they are saying. You're more likely to listen to them, to buy from them, to trust them, to respect them.

So in our lives, in the modern environment, in a competitive and distracted marketplace, it becomes increasingly critical for us to understand how do we not just talk at people and not just sell to people—how do we actually fascinate them so they want to engage with us, become involved in our products, but more importantly, enter into a relationship with us?

FELDMAN: *How do you fascinate someone?*

HOGSHEAD: There's a certain way that you communicate that adds value to other people that I call the *fascination advantage*. And when you focus on it, this is when people become most fascinated by you. This is when they listen to your communication and take action upon it.

When you successfully fascinate prospects or customers, they're focused just on you. They're not distracted. They're not thinking about their next meeting. They're not thinking about emails loading into their phone. They're definitely not thinking about the competition. They're thinking about you, and they're thinking about your message and what you have to sell.

When you're fascinating people, their brains light up, like in a state of relaxed happiness. They become in the flow. It feels effortless. Whatever message you're trying to give to them, whether it's selling a product, building a relationship, or even just having a meaningful conversation with your kids. When you're using your fascination advantage, you're far more likely to connect with people in a way that's heard and remembered and acted upon.

FELDMAN: *How does fascination work with the brain?*

HOGSHEAD: Every single human brain, throughout culture, is fascinated by the same seven triggers. I call them triggers because they are ways that the brain is instantly trained to focus on certain things. It's almost like a shortcut when you're trying to get somebody's attention. These seven different triggers are neurologically based. I'll give you a quick rundown of them.

Power is about authority and control. **Passion** is about creating an immediate emotional relationship. **Prestige** is about elevating through respect. **Mystique** is subtle and understated. It's about selectively editing what you say before you communicate. **Alarm** is about making sure that things stay on track and stay safe with detail management. **Rebellion** is about creativity and innovation, changing the game. **Trust** is about stability, reliability. It's familiar and dependable.

HOW POWER PERSONALITIES FASCINATE OTHERS IN THE WORKPLACE

Command respect

Communicate and inspire with intensity

Shape and guide people and opinions

Confront problems to clear the path for progress

Set high standards of achievement

Present with force (either subtle or energetic)

Enjoy experiences that use all of the senses

Have a participatory style that invites others to join in

One of the triggers represents the way in which your personality most naturally and authentically captures attention from other people. Your primary trigger is the way when you communicate, that you feel most comfortable and most articulate.

FELDMAN: *You say that we live in an ADD world today, how does fascination overcome this limited attention span that people seem to have these days?*

HOGSHEAD: According to some new research, the average attention span might only be nine seconds. That means that every time you introduce yourself or your message to somebody, you may only get nine seconds before they become distracted and they start focusing on something or somebody else.

When you fascinate somebody, however, not only do they listen to you but they want to become involved. They want to learn more, stay loyal, refer you, and talk about you. They want to be more than just a customer. They want to be an advocate.

This is incredibly important in trying to attract new prospects and maintaining the relationships we already have with our customers, because in an ADD world, people are always trying new things. They'll work with you for a little while, and then they'll drop you in favor of your competition. Or they'll have three different advisors all at one time for different things. It becomes really difficult to do things like sell life insurance, plan long-term investments, or help people build their financial future.

FELDMAN: *When you spoke at the annual meetings of MDRT (Million Dollar Round Table) and NAIFA (National Association of Insurance and Financial Advisors), you had the audience take the Fascination Advantage test beforehand and got a bit of surprise, didn't you?*

HOGSHEAD: Yes. The really interesting thing is when we compared the two events, they tracked very, very closely. Out of the forty-nine archetypes, they share the same top two archetypes, which obviously is statistically significant. [Archetypes are the combination of two triggers that create a personality style.]

FELDMAN: *What were the common triggers and archetypes?*

HOGSHEAD: There was an extremely strong use of Power and Prestige. When we look at the personality, that's a Power plus Prestige or Prestige plus Power, they share a lot of character traits in common. These two archetypes are named the Maestro and the Victor.

In other words, out of forty-nine archetypes, a huge percentage of them had the same two triggers, and it was so strong that the top two archetypes were the same one flipped, making them twins.

At MDRT, 7.2 percent of the group was the Maestro. At NAIFA, 8.9 percent of the group was the Maestro. Now, this is really significant. With forty-nine archetypes, hypothetically each one is going to have roughly 2 percent. But, actually, the number can be as low as .3 percent. The patterns that we see among both of these groups are very strong opinion, having a very clear idea of how to succeed and being very goal-directed. If Point A is where I am today and Point B is where I want to go, it's very clear to this group how to make that happen—how to not only envision it but how to also enact it.

This is really important for an advisor to be able to do because that's really what an advisor's core competency needs to be: seeing a goal, setting a goal, understanding how to get to the goal, and then actually realizing that goal.

FELDMAN: *If you use the Power and Prestige triggers, how can you approach people in the most effective way so that you're using these as an advantage?*

HOGSHEAD: People with power and prestige can be sometimes perceived as being a little bit intimidating because they have high standards. They have big goals. They tend to be high energy, and they can be imposing.

So it's important when these personalities first meet somebody that they understand how they're being perceived. Because, remember, the triggers test is not a test about how you see the world but about how the world sees you. And how the world sees somebody with the Power and Prestige triggers is that they're seen as ambitious, admired, focused, respected, competitive, results oriented. So the goal is not to temper those traits and tone them down. The goal is to make sure that they are channeled toward results for the client.

FELDMAN: *Was there a consistent dormant trigger, a trait they had but were not using?*

HOGSHEAD: For both of them, the highest dormant trigger was Rebellion. Rebellion is about innovation and creativity. People who use the Rebellion trigger tend to be highly entrepreneurial. They're out-of-the-box thinkers who like to be unorthodox in the way they approach situations. Advisors tend to not be like that. Advisors tend to be better at figuring out, "What's the environment? What's the goal? And what are the steps that we need to take to get there?" Not necessarily reinventing the wheel.

FELDMAN: *Does that mean advisors get out of their depth when they set up and operate their own practices?*

HOGSHEAD: Many of them are entrepreneurs. They're not entrepreneurs that are reinventing the product or reinventing the category. They are entrepreneurs who are built on relationships and on delivering for their clients. It's important for them to surround themselves with others who can supplement that.

For example, my personality archetype is the Catalyst, and the Catalyst is defined with Passion and Rebellion. So I'm great at being able to deliver big, visionary ideas for my clients, but I'm very clear that when it comes time to do the spreadsheets, the scheduling, the detailed PowerPoint follow-ups, that the rest of my team is better suited for that.

So I hire for three triggers: Trust, Alarm, and Mystique, which are best at implementation and execution. So my executive assistant is a Sustainer. The Sustainer is primary Alarm, secondary Trust. Sustainers tend to be very calm. They avoid chaos because they like to plan out every detail. They like to know exactly what's going to happen. She's very by the book. You know, like five minutes before our call started, she sends me an email and says, "Five minutes until your call. Your printouts are to your right." Everything is planned out because that's her gift, and that's why I hired her.

And for all of us, it's important for us to know our core personality advantages and how to optimize our own performance by supplementing our strengths with our team. This becomes especially critical for advisors who are the engine of their company.

FELDMAN: *How does the MDRT and NAIFA archetype stack up to other sales industries? Is it typical for top salespeople to have Power and Prestige as primary triggers?*

HOGSHEAD: No. Other sales industries tend to score higher on Passion and on Rebellion. And here's why this is different. In other sales scenarios where you have customers walking through the door, such as at a car dealership, salespeople are going to be successful if they can walk up and instantly build a connection, and they only have thirty seconds to do that. Then if that sale walks out the door, they're gone forever.

In financial services, and within the insurance industry, it's much more about building long-term patterns and being able to execute over the course of months, years, and decades. So the personalities tend to be less explosively charismatic and much more about being focused on the result that you want to achieve.

Now, one caveat that I'd like to make about everything that we're talking about right now—there's no one way to succeed. There's no one way to build relationships and communicate. So I want to be really clear that it is not that it is better if you have Power and Prestige or Power and Mystique. It has more to do with making sure that you're communicating, introducing yourself, and sharing your message in a way that's consistent with your core strengths.

So people can be extremely successful in financial services using, say, Rebellion. They are really creative and can see opportunities in the market that other people can't see, because they're able to brainstorm and think untraditionally. They can see the market's going here, but we really need to be going over there.

Sometimes you can succeed by going exactly in the opposite direction of everybody else in your industry. It's more a question of how you can apply your natural strengths to serve you, your client, and your company.

FELDMAN: *If you have similar primary triggers and secondary triggers to a client, does that create conflict?*

HOGSHEAD: It depends on the trigger. Our research shows us, for example, if you have two people who have a primary Prestige trigger, sometimes there can be a little bit of a conflict because Prestige personalities want to be able to overachieve. It's really important that you and your client have the same goals, so that you're achieving but you're on the same path and working in tandem with each other. The same is true if you were coworkers on a team, so that there isn't a power struggle going on.

On the other hand, people who had an Alarm personality are focused on details, on keeping things safe. They take a look at the whole landscape and see what can potentially go wrong. How do I make sure that we stay on budget, on track, on schedule, within the framework? So those personalities work extremely well together because they are motivated by the same things, and they add value in very similar ways. So it's very easy for the advisor to work with a client, to make sure that their money is invested conservatively, and to make sure that if the economy changes their personal financial landscape doesn't change.

FELDMAN: *The insurance and financial services business is about trust. How can you use these triggers to create trust?*

HOGSHEAD: Trust is different from all the triggers. Trust can't be created instantly. You can instantly make somebody feel passionate or curious, but you can't make somebody trust you immediately. So that's the challenge for advisors.

There are three ways to build trust without taking years to establish it.

The first is to identify patterns that you want to repeat. Trust is neurologically based on patterns. Our brain likes to see the same thing over and over again, to see the same logo, to see the same familiar face, to have the same behaviors repeated. It's why we like to wear the same things. We like to go into our closet and put on our comfortable college sweatshirt because we know it and love it. In the same way, advisors can make sure that they're very consistent. Do what they say, say what they do, and that reinforces those patterns.

The second thing that advisors can do is avoid any surprises. When people feel surprised, it causes a break in trust. Even positive surprises can make people a little bit uncomfortable because there's a break in expectations. So when you set up a meeting, don't break it. If you say you're going to be there at two, don't be there at three-thirty. If your email usually goes out on the first of the month, make sure that it goes out on the first. Your goal is to make people feel that they're safe and comfortable, that you're a familiar presence with sincerity, authenticity, and reliability that they can count on over time.

The third thing that people can do to accelerate trust is to build goals far into the future. Instead of just talking about one transaction or one product, to take things and give it a longer context, both into the future and referencing the past. So, for example, if you're trying to sell an annuity, you wouldn't want to just talk about how the transaction itself is going to happen. You want to talk about the implications far into the future and demonstrate how the annuity performs. When clients see things on a bigger time scale, they begin to think of your relationship together not as being simply a month or a year or ten years, they begin to think in terms of loyalty.

FELDMAN: *Isn't there also the danger of trust becoming boring and you lose fascination?*

HOGSHEAD: Yes. Trust can become repetitive and boring. When people become too focused on being trusted, then they start to become irrelevant, because they just do the same things over and over again. They get stuck in ruts, and this can really be the downfall for a lot of advisors that I've worked with.

Yes, they're trusted, but they are so predictable that they have trouble attracting new clients. In order to stand out in any kind of a crowded and competitive marketplace, you have to actually do just that, you have to stand out.

If you're not willing to stand out, then you need to be ready to start spending a lot more money on marketing. You will have to buy yourself new customers because you're not naturally attracting them based on your personality.

FELDMAN: *What are the most powerful triggers for consumers?*

HOGSHEAD: In bringing new customers through the door, to prospect effectively, there are three triggers: Power, Prestige, and Passion. Power and Prestige, we saw with both of the groups that we talked about. The Passion trigger helps people immediately connect with somebody through their eye contact, voice, and body language. People immediately feel close and participatory with somebody with the Passion trigger, so those are great for bringing new customers in. But keeping people over time is very different.

Keeping people over time has more to do with trust, which we just talked about. So, for financial advisors, the key is to understand how they can leverage their two triggers to not only attract new customers, either through community outreach, referrals, meeting people at events but also to keep those clients over time and have them consistently bring new business.

FELDMAN: *Can a person's triggers change over time?*

HOGSHEAD: Your personality has core competencies that are almost like your North Star. So for example, the Veiled Strength is a primary Mystique trigger with a secondary Power trigger. But maybe with their kids they would have a different way of interacting. They might be the Subtle Touch, which is Mystique plus Passion. If they were in a situation where they were unsure of what was going on, they might be the Wise Owl, which is Mystique plus Trust, and they would hold themselves back a little bit more. They wouldn't exert their opinions. People move horizontally across the primary trigger bar.

FELDMAN: *If people use different secondary triggers in different situations, do these triggers vary over time as well?*

HOGSHEAD: Yes. You're most likely to use different facets of your personality over time, staying with the same primary trigger but going across that bar. People under thirty tend to use the Passion trigger. People between thirty and fifty in their prime earning years and in an aggressive mode in their career tend to use the Power trigger. People fifty and above tend to use the Trust trigger.

What's really important to understand is that your personality has these key advantages, and when you're using them, that's when you're performing at your best. It's when you're most likely to have a breakthrough or when you're most likely to be in peak performance. It feels effortless. It feels like you don't have to put a lot of energy into the awkward and energy-draining process of being somebody that you're not.

Once you apply this core strength and build your business around it, then it's self-generative because it brings you energy. Whereas being put in a position where you're being evaluated based on triggers that are not the way that you're built to succeed, it's almost like if you were right-handed and I gave you a pencil and told you had to write with your left hand.

You could write with your left hand if you needed to, but it's not comfortable, and it's not the best use of your talents. And you're not going to reach your potential.

Final Thoughts

How Sally sees the world is as unique as her approach to personality testing. Her ability to understand how the world sees you and what about you the world finds most interesting comes with uncanny accuracy. Within hours of meeting me, she identified my personality archetype as Mystique, which was the most precise description any other personality test had ever revealed. What makes me interesting to others, Sally said, is what I don't tell them, which draws them in further.

But while a Mystique personality archetype may be good in many areas of business, it's not without some serious drawbacks. For instance, my mysteriousness also contributes to the struggles I faced in being a great communicator with my employees. My instructions and expectations were often unclear, I came to learn, and my lack of transparency left some of my employees feeling confused and even unsure of themselves in their work.

I've never been very good at being vulnerable. Like many of us, I find it uncomfortable and I justified my doing it in the workplace by telling myself it was unnecessary. Trust, I believed, was born from strength, not vulnerability. But as a leader, your employees need to know who you are before they can trust you. And without trusting you, they'll never fully commit themselves to following you.

"THE TRIGGERS TEST IS NOT A TEST ABOUT HOW YOU SEE THE WORLD BUT ABOUT HOW THE WORLD SEES YOU."

Writing more vulnerably was the first step I took to improve my communication deficiencies and gaining more trust among my workforce. Sharing company financials with my employees was another step in letting the guard down and becoming more transparent. The more I did it, the easier it became and the less vulnerable I felt doing it, which has allowed me to connect with people much more easily today.

Self-awareness is so important to transforming yourself. You can't improve yourself without knowing yourself. Likewise, you can't give others what they need without knowing who they are and what they want as well. Both are insights that Sally's method can help provide. By understanding the different types of people and their basic categories, you don't have to lump them right into the specific archetype but rather into their respective categories.

If someone's archetype is, say, Power, then what motivates them most is the feeling that they're powerful. So enable that. Enable that through your message by using visual styles and word choices that evoke power, if you're trying to attract powerful people to do business with you. You need to have some of that language in the copy, and you have to address it in your presentation with them. If someone's archetype is Alarm, then they are triggered by worry and concern, which makes them great in service. Someone who is Trust is great for sales and so on.

But the biggest benefit from Sally's work, for me, is in discovering more about who you are. When you know who you are, you can tailor the way you present yourself to more accurately reflect your personality and highlight your skills, passions, and strengths. The rewards of a greater sense of self-confidence and interpersonal likeability that kind of awareness brings are limitless.

Key Takeaways

Take time to **recognize** how others may see you. Asking friends, family, coworkers, or even a consultant to help identify your personality type will help give you a better sense of the impressions you may not realize you're projecting. What we often receive from others in our interactions with them is simply a reflection of our own projections. If you're too confident and strong-willed, for instance, you may find yourself meeting a lot of people who seem defensive, annoyed, or resistant. None will serve you well in your business. Being aware of your personality and the projections it creates is the best way to direct your interactions with others from the beginning.

Discover something that fascinates you about each person you associate with. It's that much easier to engage with them in a sincere way, thus making a deeper, longer lasting impact when you do.

People's attention spans may be as short as nine seconds. If you want to hold their attention longer than that, you *must* **fascinate** them.

Understand your own triggers or strengths, and use them. Then hire and surround yourself with people who have the important triggers that you're lacking, and delegate so all work is done well.

There are **three ways to build trust**:
1. **Repeat patterns.** Be consistent.
2. **Avoid surprises.** Even positive surprises can be jarring.
3. **Build goals far into the future.** Show things on a bigger time scale to establish commitment.

THE FINAL SPARK

There are plenty of stories about greatness. Tales abound of the enigmatic dreamer that blazed a path all their own to realize their fantasies, where success feels more like destiny than determination. You know, the inimitable, unworried genius that none of us really are but should all be striving to be anyway. That isn't me, and chances are, it isn't you either. Not even Steve Jobs could have been Steve Jobs without his large and talented team to make his ideas a reality. Yet we so often expect that we should be something exceptional right away and completely on our own—that if it isn't easy and vastly successful at the start, then it's not worth finishing. That's a lie, a myth that paralyzes too many with a fear of failure that's so heavy even the most talented and ambitious newcomers are bound to crumble under its weight.

That is not my story. My journey was not a straight shot determined solely by some supernatural aptitude or unadulterated grit. I stumbled. I failed. I doubted myself more times than I can count. In truth, my path toward becoming the business leader I am today, far from perfect as I am, was driven mostly by necessity, and the determination to prove to myself that I was worthy of professional autonomy and personal success. There were plenty of lateral moves, even steps backward, but I always wanted to push forward to a destination I could be proud of, no matter how implausible the outlook seemed to be at the time.

John Maxwell might have said it best. "Experience is not the best teacher, even though people say it is," he told me in our interview. "It's the most expensive teacher, but it's not the best teacher. Because if experience was the best teacher, as people got older, they'd automatically get better." The best teacher, according to John, is evaluated experience.

That's a truth I didn't fully understand until I began compiling this book. Over the years, I've conducted more than sixty interviews with business experts of all kinds, from scientists to self-made sales legends to marketing creatives to even a few spirituality consultants. I pored over each one, and what I learned was something of a surprise to me. Just about every interview I've ever done has, in fact, changed me.

In preparing to write this book, I had to think about who I was in my career and when I made transition points in my own life. That kind of reflection helps you reconnect with yourself, to the work you've done, and to the knowledge that you've slowly accrued over the years, often without realizing it's even there. Almost without noticing, I went from the hunter hunting alone just to survive to the guide teaching others how to hunt.

They say mastery is only achieved by teaching, but I still wouldn't call myself a master of anything. To me, there's always more to learn, and nothing can teach you more than repetition and reflection. As Chet Holmes said, "It's not about doing four thousand moves. It's doing twelve moves four thousand times." Still, repetition without reflecting on how much your form has improved does not harvest the full benefit of experience, and it certainly will not make you a good leader. Leaders, after all, must teach. You must envision better ways forward for all that follow you, and that's an impossible feat without understanding from where you've come yourself and how.

For me, that was a realization that came from a forced evaluation of the different fundamentals one always needs in their organization and discovering that it isn't enough just to know those fundamentals yourself. You have to make sure your people know them as well. You might know what to expect in business and how it will feel to progress through the obstacles, but your people don't. And growing pains are much more painful if you don't believe you're growing stronger, if you feel like you're slipping into a deep, dark pit of failed career gladiators.

There are concepts and pieces of advice in this book that everyone needs to know. Certainly there are ideas and tips I wish I had known when my journey first started, before I had to learn them the hard way or spend years researching and inquiring about to discover from others.

What we don't do as business owners and leaders nearly enough is teach what we know and share what we've learned from our failures and successes. It's easy to get wrapped up in our own job and lose touch with the notion that we're all connected, but you owe it to the people you're in connection with to inspire them and make them better. It's our job as leaders to share with them, educate them, and bring them along on our journey. Of course, in bringing them along and teaching them,

They say mastery is only achieved by teaching, but I still wouldn't call myself a master of anything. To me, there's always more to learn, and nothing can teach you more than repetition and reflection. As Chet Holmes said, "It's not about doing four thousand moves. It's doing twelve moves four thousand times." Still, repetition without reflecting on how much your form has improved does not harvest the full benefit of experience, and it certainly will not make you a good leader. Leaders, after all, must teach. You must envision better ways forward for all that follow you, and that's an impossible feat without understanding from where you've come yourself and how.

For me, that was a realization that came from a forced evalu

They say mastery is only achieved by teaching, but I still wouldn't call myself a master of anything. To me, there's always more to learn, and nothing can teach you more than repetition and reflection. As Chet Holmes said, "It's not about doing four thousand moves. It's doing twelve moves four thousand times." Still, repetition without reflecting on how much your form has improved does not harvest the full benefit of experience, and it certainly will not make you a good leader. Leaders, after all, must teach. You must envision better ways forward for all that follow you, and that's an impossible feat without understanding from where you've come yourself and how.

For me, that was a realization that came from a forced evalure's so much more they can learn and improve upon. And once they do, sharing with them what you know in an inspiring way is the only way to create a culture of education, of being better, of sharing information and building people up. What makes a good-to-great company is the people, and the more "great" people you can build up under you, the more successes you're going to achieve at the higher levels.

That's the ultimate hope I have for you. I aim to share what I've learned and documented from my journey in the hope of helping you to be inspirational in your own work and organizations. If we all find it within ourselves to inspire everyone around us to be better and share with them the tools to do so, our industry will be a better place. I'll even go so far as to say that with a little more inspiration and support from each one of us, the world is going to be a better place.

I'm not naïve. I know that's a tall order, but nothing worth doing is done easily. No matter how well we manage our time, no matter how inspiring our ideas may be, everyone still has to do the work. Growth happens one piece at a time, one brick at a time, so even more necessary than preparation is execution. Nothing has ever been built by plans alone. For your company to grow and succeed, everyone within it must understand that they have a role to play and work to do.

So share, inspire, prepare, and dare to be more than what you currently are. But most importantly, to borrow from the great Frank Kern, "Get to f---ing work!"